# Options Trading

*Pricing and Volatility Strategies and Techniques. A Crash Course for Beginners to Make Big Profits Fast with Options Trading. How to Trade to Get Your Financial Freedom*

*William L. Anderson*

indirect, which are incurred as a result of the use of information contained within this document, including, but not limited to, — errors, omissions, or inaccuracies.

# Table of Contents

Even though the agreement a business reaches with an investment bank to take them public is crucial to the IPO, it is not the only important thing that goes on in the due diligence.

# Introduction

Congratulations on downloading *Options Trading: Pricing* and Volatility Strategies and Techniques and thank you for doing so.

There are plenty of books on this subject on the market, thanks again for choosing this one! Every effort was made to ensure it is full of as much useful information as possible, please enjoy!

For someone who invests or speculates in the market, for what reason would it be advisable to know how to use options? The straightforward answer is that options can greatly improve your profit from stocks and/or offer the means to protect your portfolio. Familiarizing the amateur with call and put options as well as demonstrating some of the basic ways that options are used is the goal of this chapter.

Assume you buy a stock at $30 per share, and it rises to $33. The stock price has increased by 10%, and in like manner, you have a 10 percent profit. That is good! You may make a 100 percent profit or significantly more, for a similar 10% raise, if you buy the right option that as opposed to buying the stock. That is more than good. That is great!

# The History of the Stock Market

To understand the history of the stock market, we should have a grasp of the inner workings of a stock exchange first—specifically the bid-ask spread that also influences prices of shares. The bid-ask spread is a sort of register that consolidates the demand and supply of stock in a central position. On the one hand, it allows people who need to buy stocks to place an order of the number and price of shares they intend to buy. On the other, it gives the sellers an opportunity to list the number of shares they intend to sell, as well as the target price for them. The final price of the stock depends on whether the buyer is willing to settle for the price of the buyer or whether the buyer is able to buy the stocks at their listed price. The laws of demand and supply also come into play, with buyers being forced to increase their purchase price when the competition is higher and sellers accepting a lower price for their stocks if there are not enough buyers to drive demand and price up.

Now, the stock exchange facilitates this conversion of ownership from the seller to the buyer by bringing them together in one platform. It is essentially a platform comprising of stockbrokers where they congregate to perform the business of exchanging (buying and selling) stocks. But who exactly runs the stock exchange? The stock exchanges as they currently exist were founded so long ago that the issue of who owns them seems immaterial. For the most part, the stock exchange is just the building or platform on which brokers buy and sell. The most important aspect of the stock exchange is the stocks that are listed in it. And because companies only list where they can be sure of attracting investors (stockholders), this is a very important aspect of their operations. It is no surprise, therefore, that the oldest bourses were started as corporations by stockbrokers to facilitate the exchange of securities among themselves.

The stock market has had a long and eventful history, one that is almost as long as the banking industry, by far the oldest financial institution still surviving today.

## 1100s–1400s

The earliest versions of the stock market were rather different from the bourse as we know it today. In France, the country of origin for these early stock exchanges, courretiers de change agents oversaw the agricultural debts issued by banks to farmers all over the state. They could swap and renegotiate these debts, an equity exchange that formed the foundation for the current stock market. Over time, the business of exchanging debts grew, and these men expanded to new markets, including government securities. As the first stockbrokers, the Venetian courretiers de change established stocks as a legitimate way for "common" people to make money in the financial markets.

Interestingly, these men carried on a system of cross-transactions with each other, buying debt and equity of each other based on risk and various other factors. Because they represented different banks in the debt issuance and collection sector, this interlinkage would later evolve to become the present-day interbank lending system, whereby banks issue each other with cheaper short-term loans. The people involved in this trade were mostly commodity traders, with the value of commodities changing hands but not the commodities themselves. This was a virtualization of the business functions that was way ahead of its time at the time.

The merchants of Venice started trading in government securities in the early thirteenth century. They were soon followed by banks in Verona, Genoa, Florence, and Pisa as it became evident that government securities presented a wonderful investment opportunity. Trading between the merchants was done by word of mouth and handwritten agreements. The extent of organized trading was limited to the houses of prominent traders where many of these courretiers de change could congregate and negotiate terms and conduct their transactions.

From France, the development of the securities market moved to Belgium and Netherlands, where traders started stock markets in Antwerp, Bruges, Ghent, and Rotterdam between the 1400s and the 1500s. In Antwerp, a clan of traders named the Van der Beurze family established a hub for stock traders to exchange equities, forming the first formalized stock market, except it still traded in agricultural debts, commodities, and government bonds. The concept of private companies using the stock markets to raise money had not yet been born.

## 1500s–1700s

In the meantime, before the first publicly-traded company made it into the bourse, England joined in the "stock" trading enterprise. As usual, government securities were the main commodities traded, but debts and commodities also changed hands. By this time, as European civilizations continued to expand, there was a stock market in pretty much every country that had a banking industry. Business ownership also started to change, with partnerships and corporations becoming increasingly popular as businessmen recognized the profit of combining their financial muscle. New philosophies of a business organization birthed the limited liability system of business organization and paved the way for the modern conglomerate.

The first publicly traded company would emerge from an unexpected area: risk. At a time when the Western world was discovering the rest of the world and venturing out to explore it, merchant ships were making many traders extremely rich. Explorers had discovered the West Indies as a land filled with business opportunities and tremendous riches, but the sea routes they took exposed them to piracy, with numerous voyages turning up zero returns because a ship was ransacked at sea. In fact, losing a ship meant that the trader, who had put up the money for the voyage, including the commodities to be bartered for gold and other treasure, wound up losing a ton of money.

To reduce the risk of losing a merchant ship at sea, a group of traders formed the East India Company, with each owning a portion of the assets but shielded from personal liability for any losses suffered beyond their investment in that particular expedition. This format of overseas trading quickly caught on. By keeping one's eggs in separate baskets, so to say, traders could have one out of three or four of their invested ships lost at sea and still end up making some money from the transaction.

A shareholding in a company became more and more liberalized; the Dutch East India Company became, in 1602, the first publicly-traded company. The shares of the company were listed on the Amsterdam Stock Exchange. Every share was entitled to an equal percentage of the proceeds of the company's profits. However, the trading of shares was not done in dedicated exchange houses. For example, the business of the New York Stock Exchange was conducted in coffee shops. Brokers would meet in coffee shops and conduct their business there, but this soon proved to be too ineffective, and the business of trading shares was moved into the stock exchanges.

The systems that even today moderate stock trading were put in place back then, enabling the traders to physically identify the person with the shares they wanted, approach them, and negotiate to buy them off. The counter was soon discovered to be a better alternative to tracking down traders with a particular stock. People intending to sell would just list their shares at the counter, and people wanting to buy would place their orders at the counter. An easy and effective system of centralized control was established, but having a centralized buy/sell counter meant that the market forces of demand and supply were also let loose. Someone with stock could wait until so many orders had been placed that they could name their price, however exorbitant, and get a buyer.

# Chapter 1

# Financial Contracts

## The Basic Concept of Options

### Choosing a Brokerage Account

When selecting an online broker for your options trading, there's one essential principle: There is a replacement for options experience. Obviously, make your own decisions. Because somebody loves a broker doesn't mean you will—or that you need to utilize them. What you do need to do, in any case, is build up a plan for assessing the brokers you consider, so you'll guarantee that the one you eventually pick offers the features you need— and certainly require.

Luckily, assembling such a "shopping list of services" isn't very hard. I won't say it is "as simple as 1-2-3," however, it surely is "as easy as 1 to 10"— the following ten things being the least number of capabilities you should request in any online options broker you pick.

# Factors to Review When Choosing a Broker

1. **The standard of the trading software.** For online traders, this is the most basic issue, and it takes various inquiries to decide exactly what number of features is incorporated—and how great they are. These include:

- Is the software user-friendly; easy to comprehend and simple to utilize?
- Can I get it on a disk or would I be able to download it from the internet?
- Is it hard to install on my PC? Will I require help?
- Does it require any unique equipment or communications highlights, for example, high-speed modems, specialty internet browsers or DSL lines—with the end goal to make it work proficiently?
- Does it incorporate adequate pricing and logical, analytical tools for my requirements?
- If not, is it built to be effortlessly incorporated into independent quotation frameworks and analytical services? Let's assume this is the case, are there any exceptional pricing plans?
- Is satisfactory customer documentation given—both printed and online—to enable both to understand the framework and manage any technical issues?

- Is it attractive to look at—and, in the event that I don't like it, would I be able to change such things as size or color or display? (This may appear to be unimportant, yet in case you will be an active trader, you might take a look at it on and off for six or seven hours every day. In this manner, you don't need something you hate on a stylish premise.)

2. **The simplicity of order entry and the speed of transmission to the trade.** This is additionally critical for active traders, who might put in heaps of requests and need the procedure to be as programmed as possible. Some key things to ask:

- What number of fields on the order-entry screen do I need to fill in to put in a request?
- Do I really need to type in all the data, or will the software import it from the logical or pricing screens in the event that I need?
- Do I need to manually go back to the firm's order screen, or would I be able to get to it by tapping on the screens given by incorporated trading partners?
- Does the program send the order to the trade when I submit it, or does it need to be prepared elsewhere inside the firm first?

- Do I need to indicate the trade where the order is sent, or does the program shop around at the best cost and course the order as needs are?
- Do I put orders specifically through your software, or must I have a browser to get to your framework?
- Can orders be entered at night-time, for execution the next day—or just while the market is open?
- Do you additionally have a site—and, provided that this is true, would I be able to put orders from the site and also through the software?

3. **Quality of service to options traders.** Still another area where you have to make a few important inquiries, including:

- Are there independent order screens for stocks and options?
- If not, can the order screen be personalized to take into account options traders?
- Are the options quotes given in the order screen constantly or deferred?
- In the event that you call up an option chain; is it a real-time preview, or a delayed collation of last prices? Furthermore, is it spread out in an orderly way, or do you need to search for the option you need?

- Does the option-pricing framework give you access to current bids and offers, or simply last trading prices? What about volume numbers? Open interest?

- Does the framework include multi-option strategies, for example, spreads, and give you a chance to order them as a unit?

- If so, does it charge one commission for such orders—or survey fees for every option in the combination?

- Will the framework settle for stop and stop-limit orders on options? What about stops and buy orders that are dependent upon the price of the basic asset?

- Do any of the incorporated quote services spend specialize in options?

- If yes, will their program give me a chance to punch in trade parameters and screen for good trading chances?

- Does the brokerage firm's program have any comparable services to assist me with options analysis?

4. **Timely executions and confirmations.** The broker's order entry program ought to give guide access to the electronic trading frameworks of the suitable trades and, once your trades qualify for programmed execution, report back a confirmation in few seconds—ideally to an area of the order-entry screen where you can quickly observe that you got your fill. In the event that the trade doesn't qualify

the bill for programmed execution, it ought to show up in a corner on your screen intended to give you a chance to monitor your working orders.

5. **Ability of the framework to deal with high-volume circumstances.** The broker's database ought to have the adequate reserve processing capacity to deal with additional overwhelming order stream—and the firm ought to have a framework set up to manage quick economic situations as successfully as possible. (No firm is flawless when such circumstances occur, yet they ought to make an attempt to at the very least—not simply hurl their hands and say, "Sorry" or "Too bad!")

6. **Commission costs.** Numerous traders would put commissions much higher on the list than No. 6; however, our reasoning is unique. To mind: What great are low commissions in the event that you get lousy prices, moderate executions and terrible (or no) benefit? Ensure the broker gives you all that you need—and require—and don't stress on the chance that it cost a couple of additional dollars. You'll likely influence it up on your trades, at any rate. Do, in any case, demand that the broker's fees, at any rate, be competitive; you need to pay for what you get—not pay to get gouged. Additionally, make sure to get some information about possibly

precarious things covered up underneath a guarantee of low commissions—e.g., a commission rate of $1 per option won't help you a whole lot if the firm forces a $50 least on each order.

7. **Customer support.** Very important! It's a must-have—ideally by telephone, not only online, by email or through a self-improvement menu on the site (in spite of the fact that it's pleasant to have those choices too). Likewise, see if support is accessible simply amid business hours — or terribly, just when the market's open. Your goal is to guarantee that the help services will be accessible on the occasions you really require help.

8. **Backups for order execution in case of technical issues.** As we'll talk about in one moment, there will be times when things turn out badly—even with the best broker and the most superb programming. In the event that it occurs within trading hours, your broker must have a backup framework to manage it. That implies having enough telephone lines and in-house individuals to deal with client calls and the sudden flood of disconnected order stream. All things considered, no trader who frantically needs to escape a position 30 minutes before the end wants to call his broker and hear a tinny, computer voice: "All agents are at presently occupied;

however, your call is vital to us. Please stay on the line; a delegate will be with you in roughly 45 minutes"— soon after you've lost your shirt!

9. **Simple access to account data.** Trading capability isn't the sole key to accomplishment in options trading—money management is similarly vital. But it's difficult to deal with your money in the event that you can't easily access the status of your account. With a decent broker software program, you ought to have the capacity to get to all key data—including open positions and their values, balances, total equity, available equity, result of recent trades, and profit/loss statements (ideally, the ones you can ask for by period or on a year-to-date premise). The perfect framework will likewise play out the majority of the math and the greater part of the accounting capacities for you.

10. **Security of individual and financial data.** Numerous individuals fear to do anything online in light of the fact that they fear a hacker or another person will discover excessively about them, take their personalities—or, surprisingly more terrible, take their money. Insubstantial part, these fears are unreasonable—particularly inside the frameworks of America's financial services systems, which were planned in view of security and had unique

assurances, set up. Therefore, most brokerage frameworks are as secure as it's presently conceivable to make them. All things considered, it never hurts to make an inquiry.

## Strive For the Perfect Choice

I said the broker shopping procedure would be "as basic as 1 through 10"— yet, with all the sub-questions listed, it, in fact, got more complex. All things considered, it's just for your advantage.

Clearly, not very many firms will have the capacity to give the affirmations you need regarding all of the worries just made reference to—yet, you ought to make progress toward perfection. The more things you need to consider with respect to the "mechanics" of online trading, the more opportunities will be made available for you to end up diverted and falter as you move along the way to options achievement.

Keeping that in mind, survey the 10-shopping process listed above over once again, and choose what highlights you completely should have—and which you might have the capacity to live without. At that point, when the forthcoming brokerage firm says something isn't accessible, you'll know in a split second if it's enough to make you leave.

In case you're a genuinely new trader, you may likewise need to check whether the broker offers any close to home, one-on-one investment counsel, or proposes trading chances to customers. Relatively few online firms do, yet in the event that such things are important to you, it doesn't hurt to inquire. You may, at any rate, get a referral to a partnered warning service or data site that can help give some trading thoughts.

This enables a client to manage a prepared options broker to deal with orders and questions. The commission charges are not quite the same as the online rates—yet the value included by having a live broker will most likely be worth the expense in case you're simply taking in the trading ropes.

Obviously, the essence of online trading is accomplishing direct access to the trades so you can perform your transactions precisely like the experts. In this way, you should attempt to wean yourself from the requirement for broker help before going online—or as fast as possible from thereon.

# Chapter 2 - Forward Pricing

Low margins can be very useful when trading. To use them successfully, they must be integrated into the overall pattern. The basic idea is to enter the market as soon as it breaks out of the state of equilibrium that exists. If the price rises sharply from this point on and then falls back down there, an increase in demand is expected. This is a classic double bottom. In combination with the Accumulation / Distribution, this becomes the basis for an interesting trading approach. Choose only the trades in the direction of the thrust. Place stops at the opposite end of the short bar.

## Trading Beams with Large Margins

A wide-span bar can be either bullish or bearish, depending on where it appears in the formation. If it appears at the end of a buy peak, then it is to be classified as bearish, at the break from a formation, however positive. Most beams with a large span are followed directly by a correction beam. The buy zone is in the lower half of the bar, and the profit-taking area is located at around 50% to 100% of the span above the high of the bar. Of course, this only applies to short-term traders. The course tends to be varied, with a short track following a long bar. Of course, this is not always the case, and the definition of a wide-span bar is subjective. This is where the art of chart reading comes into play. This ability can only be learned by analyzing many charts over the years.

## Purchase Zones

The buy zone describes the lower half of a push. While the relapses are causing the price to rise, the buying zone also moves upwards. In these areas, you should look for opportunities to get started. Before you open your position, you should know where to set the stop and set a price target. Mark the buy zone, the stop loss and the area of the price target in the chart. Do not chase after a quick course! Among the countless stocks, there is always a good candidate for a better start. Opt for a boarding area. The following steps could help:

1. Buy only in the purchase zones.
2. Place your stop loss immediately after opening your position.
3. Be sure to close the position when you reach the winning zone. Is this done by means of a stop, or are you simply selling? Any possibility is a compromise: if you sell, the price could rise even higher. Waiting for the stop to be triggered will often result in significant portions of the potential win.

The following options are available:

- Make the stop tighter.
- Close only half the position. So, your decision is only half wrong or half correct.
- Close your position at the first sign that the supply outweighs the demand.
- Use a shorter time frame to set the stop. For example, if you trade on a daily chart, choose a 30-minute chart to place your stop more accurately.

# The Stop

If you do not know what you are risking, you risk everything. There is no stop-loss option that is equally satisfactory for everyone. Everyone has to find out for himself which ratio of risk to the potential profit he feels comfortable with. Here are some suggestions for placing stop orders:

1. Three ticks below the low of the last or penultimate fulcrum

2. An average range below the closing price or the low of the day on which the purchase was made

3. 50% of the breakout or break-in after opening the day after entering the position. This stop works especially well when combined with the other possible stops. For example, a value sometimes opens below a stop at a level, which then turns out to be the low of the day. We like to see it move about eight ticks or half the span of the previous bar after opening.

4. Three ticks below the lower low or lower end of the last two bars

5. Close the position after three bars, if it is not yet in the profit zone.

6. Release the trade and try to exit without loss if the trade runs too far against you after the opening and your stop is not triggered. Do not think about a possible profit

anymore. Their only interest is the stopping and preservation of your capital.

It is of utmost importance to always have a good plan ready for your investment. When opening a position, ask yourself if this is a long-term investment for five or ten years or not. Then you should not panic in the face of short-term price fluctuations. Are you a trader? Unfortunately, many people set their exit point or stop loss according to the following criteria:

1. The stop-loss is at a point where the losses are already huge.
2. The stop is based on the general market situation. If the whole market collapses, my positions will be closed.
3. As soon as everyone is frantically trying to close their positions in my stock quickly, then I sell too.
4. Any analyst or broker says you should get out now. That reminds me of a story.

A few years ago, I had the honor to come on the Mark Haynes show. I was invited by CNBC. Mark introduced me as an expert on the futures market. He asked me how the gold would develop. I replied that I knew exactly how the gold price would continue to behave. But before I answer that question, I'd have to make the audience aware that until now, I've only been 23% right, and I'm on the rise, so the main danger is that sometimes I could be right.

And if that were known, I added, and then I could barely pay for the bus ride to my house. Of course, after this interview, CNBC tried to select the invited guests in a better manner.

The moral of the story is that you should beware of people who have all the answers to all questions. If you want to be a trader, then you must realize that success must be hard-won and that you will pursue a monster all your life that you will never master. But maybe you learn to live with it, and you get more than you give.

# Profit Taking

If you have a long position and the price goes into profit, then you can protect your profit by:

- Best selling
- Sell when a closing price is below an opening.
- Sell when the price falls after the opening by half the average range.
- Set the stop below the previous day's low.
- Sell when the price closes below the two previous closing prices and below the opening.
- Sell at the third strong positive bar of the next smaller time frame. For example, if the price breaks into the profit

zone on the weekly chart, then you sell after the third consecutive day in a row.

## Anticipation

The following factors are important in anticipating the completion of a pattern or reversal. You can build parts of a position at an early stage before all criteria are met. Remember: The stated goal is to make profitable trading and not to be in the market at 90% of all price moves. Learn to settle for small pieces of the market. Either you secure your profits by means of a best-order, or you sell at the first sign that the supply exceeds the demand.

1. The seven possible times to anticipate a pattern are:
2. The closing price of the bar, if a short spread indicates a low supply or low demand.
3. An opening course in the direction of completing the pattern.
4. An outbreak after opening in the direction of completing the pattern.
5. An outbreak after 30 minutes towards the completion of the pattern.
6. The course is midway through the opening and in the direction of completing the pattern.
7. At the closing price if the pattern is fully developed.

8.  For a correction movement after completing the pattern. For many patterns, it can be seen that the price will fall back into the buy zone, but the pattern will be completed above the buy zone. Then it has to be decided on a case-by-case basis which measure is the right one.

## The Time-Break-Out Rule

A common approach is to trade the breakout from the first 30-minute bar, with the stop loss at the other end of this bar. This approach has been tested using S & P's market data over 14 years. Trading according to this rule leads to huge losses. It should be noted that this method has been profitable in recent years. But one must always keep in mind the fact that how dangerous it can be, if too short a test period is chosen to check a method. When entering a position, the 30-minute rule may be useful, but as with most tools, isolated use will not work.

## Price Gaps

Normally, a positive price gap is considered a sign of strength and a buy signal. In verifying this assumption, it turned out that the exact opposite is true. The review was based on two methods:

1.  Sale with a positive price gap.

2. Sale on a positive price gap, but only if the price falls back to the previous day high.

For purchases, the opposite applies. Both approaches were tested by computer without stops and as day trades. The second approach turned out to be almost twice as successful as the first. It is used approximately 60 times a year per future. The course must go in your direction before doing anything. This signal provides a clear market advantage, but in most cases does not make up for the fees and slippage. But when combined with other filters and more meaningful stop management, this is a valuable addition to your trading arsenal. Coincidentally, the review found that this could be a profitable trading system for bonds.

This pattern is very similar to a pattern developed by Larry Williams called Oops. The starting point is the same, but we do not know which entry and exit criteria were used by him. The information can be reused as follows:

1. The signal is likely to be more reliable if the price has already gone one way and the expected end of that price movement is within range. Then this could be a good way to realize profits and perhaps build up counter positions.
2. Other ideas are:

- Watch out for introductory signals on reverse movements of the last closing price, several previous closing prices, and several previous highs and lows.
- Consider setting a half-span stop after boarding.
- Watch price gaps above or below a cluster of close closing prices.
- Look for a reversal after half the gap in the price gap before opening a position.

These simple computer tests will tell you quickly whether such an opening with a price gap will give you a technical advantage in view of past price developments or not. Larry Williams and Toby Crabel have made a name for themselves in this field. Whole volumes could be filled solely with the study of price movements in relation to the opening and the movement away from the opening price.

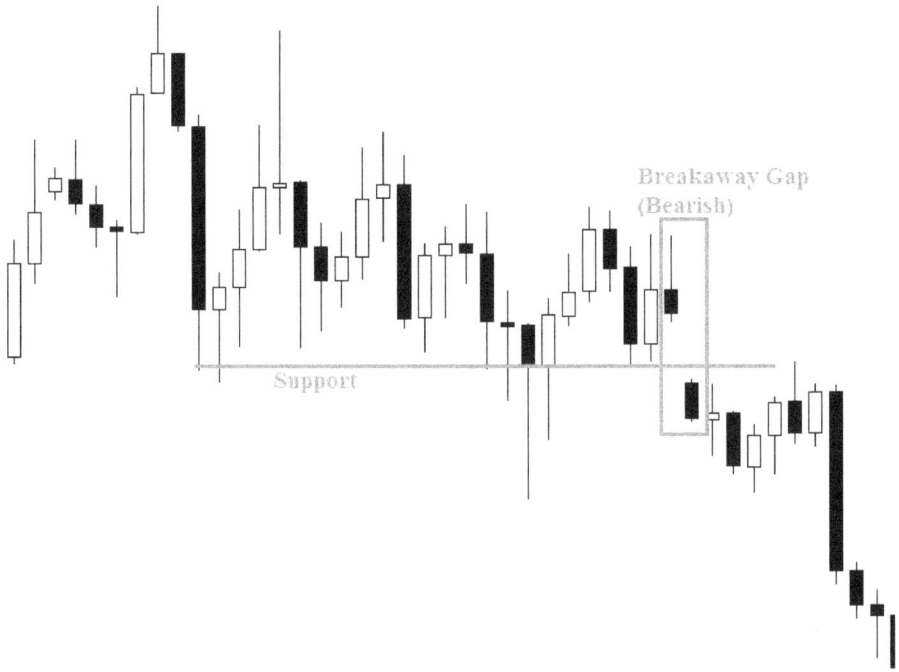

Breakaway Gap
(Bearish)

Support

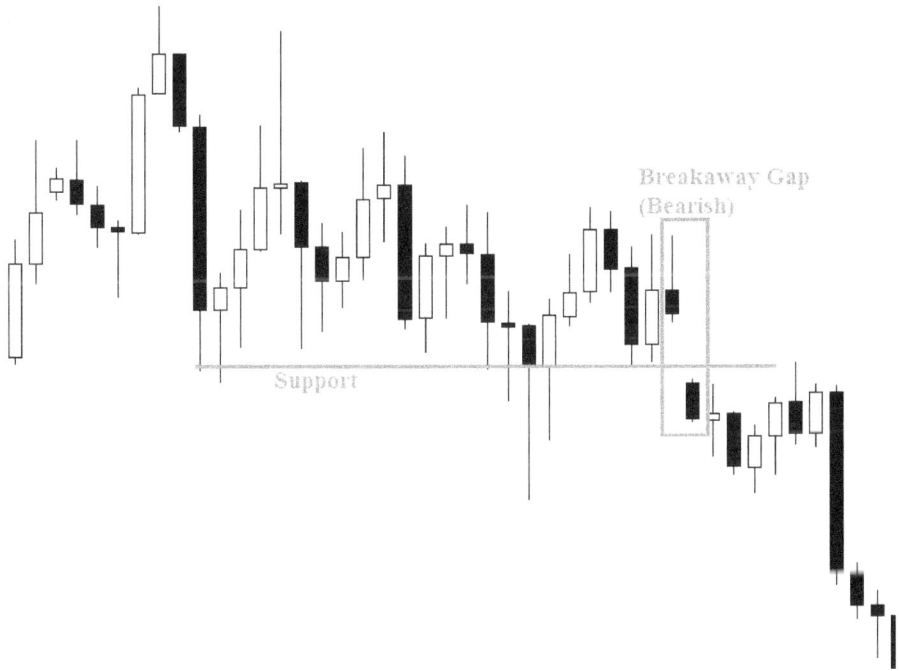

Breakaway Gap
(Bearish)

Support

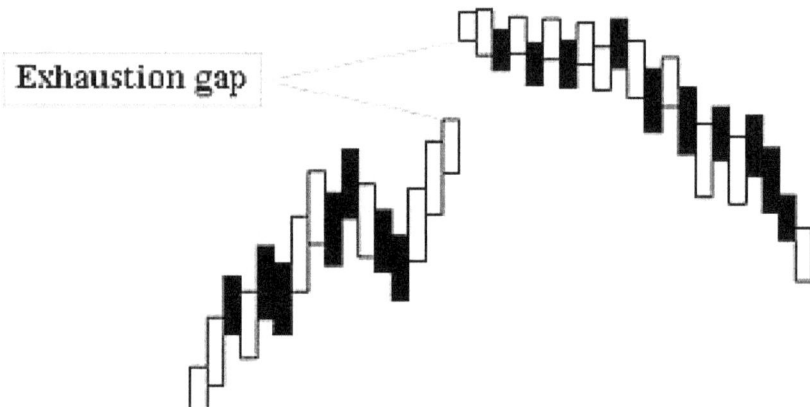

Exhaustion gap

## Channels and Trend Lines

The information in this chapter will help you identify the most **advantageous** opportunities for trades, as it is about identifying smaller and larger channels. This is especially important when it comes to trading decisions on reversal or continuation patterns. The use of simple trend lines, combined with some basics of wave theory as a starting technique, is also covered. Some of the methods in this section are not the same as transferring them to a computer system, but the ideas that are discussed will certainly be very clear if you look at a chart with the registered lines and channels. From this, a systematic approach can be developed.

One of the most valuable tools for the trader is trend lines. Many use indicators that are calculated by a sophisticated computer program. Roughly speaking, all these indicators try to answer the same question: how much is the market overbought or oversold? Simple trendlines with a few extra rules can be used most effectively in timing your trades. Learn to read the charts, not just the indicators. So far, we have not found an indicator that tells us that there has just been a kink or a jump and that we should do better when we are in the market. The drawback is that the price drops to a new low below a pivot or support finds no-bid, and then rises aggressively. The jumping occurs when the course suddenly rises to a new high above a turning point, finds no demand and quickly falls back. These procedures are discussed in more detail further in the book.

## Trend Line and Parallel Movements

A major high on a pivot is followed by at least two deeper pivot points before it hits a new high (and vice versa at lows). The main trend line connects two main highs or main lows that are at pivot points. The parallel motion is a parallel line that passes through the main pivot point. The goal of the movement is where the price hits the parallel line again, that is, the boundary of the trend channel. Smaller trend channels are constructed by connecting lesser pivot points. The target range is the parallel trend line, the other side of the trend channel.

# Trading With the 0-2 Line

The following setup: The market is experiencing a surge of strong demand but is currently in the correction phase. If wave C remains above the level of the lower pivot point A, then the purchase takes place when the 0-2-line breaks through. If the pivot point C is below half of A, then you should wait with a possible entrance to wave 4.

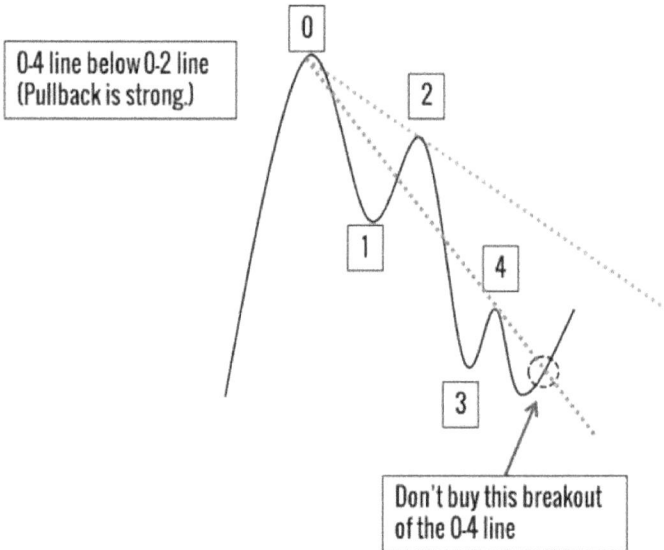

The trade-in parallel moves, the 0-2 and 0-4 lines requires some subjective decisions. The logical sequences that would be necessary for programming in a computer system are enormously complex and difficult. Still, the rules are pretty simple, and entry and exit points are easy to determine. You do not need a computer for that.

## Trend Lines and the Four-End System (TL4S)

This is a simple system that can be followed without a computer. You just have to be able to assess the trend correctly and decide whether the profit potential is worth the risk taken. The setup for the purchase (the opposite applies in the case of sale):

1. Always act in the direction of the trend.
2. Drag a trend line that joins the last two top pivot points.
3. In the last 20 days, two or more rising or equal high lower pivot points formed.

Buy on a price move, though

- The closing price is above the four previous closing prices.
- The span is above average.

The stop is below the last lower pivot point. Sell immediately if there are signs of a false signal or outbreak. Push the stop further upwards to the breakeven point, as soon as you have some leeway, so that the risk of a loss is banned, and the fees are covered. The evaluation of the margin is at your discretion, but the following suggestion may help: Place the stop just below the low of the entry day as soon as the high of the entry day is exceeded by half the span.

## Realize Your Profits

1. When reaching the target area.
2. In a breakthrough of the four-closing trend line against the trend direction.
3. In the event of an outbreak halfway through the opening after the price enters the sales area.

These are all suggestions. The basic idea is to break the position as soon as the first signs become apparent, that the supply exceeds demand or that a buying peak is emerging (in the case of shorts, of course).

The trend channel system

If the price falls on the lower channel line, buy/sell at the first positive indication of a trend change:

- Purchase at a higher opening
- Buy after the 11:30 am Rule (mid-day course above the opening)
- Buy on a reversal day
- Buy with smaller reversal patterns
- Buy at the correction

- Shorter-term time frame. Observe the 30-minute chart and buy near the parallel line (on the daily chart) at the first sign of strength in the shorter time frame.

# Types of Options Traders and Trading Styles

Most would agree that, in spite of the fact that the fundamental options trading are not extraordinarily hard to understand, there is a great deal of information that should be understood before you probably feel okay to start. The basics are generally clear; you need to know what it entails, the advantages, what the risks are and how options truly function.

One of the few different things to know is the diverse trading styles that can be utilized along with the distinctive sorts of an options trader.

As a rule, traders can be grouped into two. To start with, you have the professionals, those that typically work for big financial institutions, trading specifically in the interest of those institutions or for the benefit of customers. These professionals can likewise fill the job of market makers.

Also, you have private people that trade entirely for themselves utilizing their own capital and for the most part, they trade from home. A few people trade full-time, depending on their profits as their essential source of pay, while others trade temporarily while additionally having a principal work.

Day trading is a style that can be utilized for practically any type of financial trading, including forex, futures, and stocks, and in addition, options. Customarily, it was a style utilized just by financial institutions and professionals. However, it has turned out to be known among locally established traders as well. There are various purposes for this. However, it's to a great extent because of the impact of online technology which has made it less difficult to make financial transactions rapidly and furthermore expanded the measure of information and data that can be gained access to.

Day trading usually includes exploiting little price movements, the way you utilize leverage when buying and selling option makes them an especially reasonable financial instrument for this style.

## What Does Day Trading Options Entail?

The fundamental idea of day trading options is straightforward; the idea is that you make various transactions during the day with the intention of making fast profits. The general standard is that you close the entirety of your open positions by the close of business, so you know precisely where you remain toward the day's end. With this style, you can buy and sell a wide range of options and can utilize various diverse strategies.

A few trades can include taking a position early in the day and closing it close at day end while others may include buying and selling options contracts in a few minutes. This depends to an extent on what openings you find and what kind of strategies you are utilizing.

The interesting thing about this style is that it is, in fact, at least, feasible to make fast profits many times during the day. Those that utilize this style successfully know about discovering openings that have a good chance of selling positive returns. Obviously, there will never be an assurance that every single open door will be profitable.

This style is sometimes referred to as active trading, and you do need to be active to utilize it successfully. You should have the capacity to spot open doors for-profit and respond rapidly. The fundamental rule is to exploit little price movements in the hidden security of options, so timing is imperative. A couple of minute's postponement can possibly mean a botched chance or no less than a decrease in the potential profits.

# Who Uses This Style?

As said earlier, day trading any sort of financial instrument used to be done just by the master professional that worked for banks and other financial institutions, and possibly the periodic private investor. Nowadays, in any case, it's a style that is supported by a lot of private investors, and it's proceeding to be known by people. The apparent advantages of having the capacity to make fast profits, rather than clutching investments with a view to making a return later have brought about it winding up essentially more standard.

Day trading options, specifically, makes it achievable to make great returns from generally little sums using leverage. The objective is to profit by little movements in the prices of stocks, and other hidden securities and options can increase the potential gains from such losses.

Options are amazing means whenever utilized effectively, and there are numerous traders that profit simply through making fast trades over the span of every single day. It should be noted that utilizing leverage can likewise increase potential losses, and there are risks involved.

The fundamental point, essentially, is that basically anybody can be involved with day trading; you don't have to work for a big financial association, and you don't require a large amount of money to begin. Anybody that is ready to dedicate the needed time to fully realize what they have to know and after that, examine the markets every day to highlight openings, will eventually be successful. All things considered, it is not encouraged for a total amateur.

## Guidance for Day Trading Options

There are some recommendations that anybody keen on day trading options ought to know about. As a matter of importance, it's serious and time-devouring, and you should be ready for what it entails. It's unrealistic to execute this style very well except if you have time and a dedicated personality to devote yourself to watching the markets for the duration of the day.

You should be cautious every time and be prepared to act when it's a perfect time. In that regard, you additionally require the capacity to investigate circumstances rapidly and carry out your trades as need be. In the event that you believe you cannot adapt to the requests, you ought to think about different styles.

You should have a deep insight and understanding of the different strategies that can be used, know how to use them, and when to utilize them. You should be exceptionally disciplined and have the capacity to keep feelings out of the situation. You also need to be ready to accept the risks that come with it (if it happens).

You can, to a certain level, reduce the risk that you are presented to by utilizing spreads and stop-loss orders to limit losses. However, there will be risk included. Risks are especially high when the market is unpredictable, even though unstable market conditions give the most profitable situations.

Even though you don't really require a large amount of capital to begin, you ought to have sufficient money to cover yourself if a few traders don't go right or if there are long unprofitable days depending on the amount you are hoping to make. You additionally need to make transactions at the suitable level for the spending you have; numerous beginner day traders become bankrupt basically in light of the fact that they come up short on capital due to not dealing with their money accurately.

It is true that money can be made from day trading options. It is in no way simple, however, and you truly need the correct aptitudes, devotion and a sense of responsibility. Should you feel you are prepared to give it a go, it is a smart thought to paper trade for a short time before really utilizing genuine money. This will get you used to what it entails and give you some signs concerning whether you have the correct character and ability to make it work.

# Options Brokers for Day Trading Options

Picking the correct broker is an imperative choice for an options day trader. Specifically, there are two things that you truly require: the capacity to put orders immediately when you recognize a chance and low commissions. Since the plain idea of this style is tied with responding rapidly, any postponement in directing your broker can have great consequence. You will likewise be making a lot of trades, so low commissions are considerably more essential than for different styles.

The sole intelligent decision is to utilize an online broker. Online brokers will, in general, be the least expensive in terms of commissions, and you can submit your requests substantially more rapidly than if you needed to make a telephone call to your broker.

# Chapter 3

# Options Trading Simulators

You've most likely heard everything before: If it's too good to be true, then it probably is, and trading options without risking your money definitely falls into that class. Conventional investors and specialists alike would reveal to you that there's no such thing as risk-free trading – which is valid, obviously (can't contend with the specialists!).

However, note that you can learn and practice options trading without putting any money hanging in the balance. Market novices and prepared investors alike can utilize virtual options trading to increase significant experience and test trading strategies without risking any hard-earned money.

I will prescribe the best platforms accessible online to open your options trading account with.

## Free Options Trading?

Virtual options trading — or paper trading—includes investing virtual money in business sectors defined by different online platforms. With a paper trading simulator, you have the chance to work on trading hands-on with zero risks.

You've most likely inquired about options trading and may definitely know fundamentals, yet the buck doesn't stop there. A few people would state that you can hop into the universe of options trading promptly. However, I exceptionally advise against that. The complexity can be scary for any dimension investor.

For entry-level traders, free trading simulators are the ideal place to begin: you'll have the chance to practice and handle the fundamentals in a risk-free condition, and most will likewise incorporate accommodating assets in the event that you lose all sense of direction in the dialect of options trading. It's likewise incredible for experienced traders alike, as you can be permutated and masters your strategies and approach before taking your risk in genuine trading.

A considerable number of these trading platforms are free. Not only do you not risk losing your well-deserved money, but you also don't need to spend a penny to practice virtual options trading. What else would you want?

# The Best Free Paper and Virtual Options Trading

Trading simulators have been utilized in the financial markets to prepare younger traders. Indeed, even before the business sectors turned out to be overwhelmingly electronic, the utilization of basic, offline trading amusements, for example, Liar's Poker to instruct the basic aptitudes of trading was at the center of many preparing programs. Financial market simulators are risk-free and a charming method to learn!

Be that as it may, most present-day simulators are a long way from flawless. Some simply offer 'phantom' market information whereupon 'phantom' trades can be executed. This is limiting on the grounds that the simulator is just accessible when the basic market is open. What's more, a couple of simulators give the client much feedback on their execution or about how to make strides. Truth be told, most simulators are simply simulators; they make no endeavor to really show the client the financial markets.

Here's a survey of my most loved platforms to rehearse options trading online. All are appropriate for both learning and expert traders, so pick the platform that best suits every one of your needs, and registers to get a practice trading account.

- **Investopedia.** Obviously – you've known about Investopedia; While Investopedia is more popular as a result of its huge measure of instructive assets utilized in fund and trading, the site likewise brags of its simple-to-use stock simulator. You begin with $100,000 worth of virtual money to invest, and you can even view different options chains through this platform. While the simulator as of now has some valuable aides accessible in it, the Investopedia site is as of now an extraordinary asset for every one of your inquiries when you feel overpowered with the trading dialect you may not be comfortable with.

- **Options Industry Council.** The Options Industry Council trading simulator furnishes clients with real-time analyses of markets – considering their current economic situations. This is ideal for the individuals who are anxious to get the hang of trading options in the current financial condition today. The simulator is totally free, and you can decide to use the accessible information from the simulator, or you could enter your very own information to work with. The OIC simulator isn't as complete contrasted with next couple of simulators I will specify. Be that as it may, once more, in case you're a learner, this simulator may be the opportune place to begin.

- **Market Watch.** Market Watch is prominent among experienced clients and even specialists of the market – likely in light of the fact that Market Watch frequently opens challenges where the best trader gets featured on an article on their site. In case you're an amateur, MarketWatch can likewise work for you, as you can still trade alone – without the stress of rivalry – utilizing virtual cash and real-time data access. Their primary site additionally contains the most recent updates in financial and investment-related news, which can be valuable for your upgrade execution in the game.

- **Thinkorswim PaperMoney.** Thinkorswim is apparently the best options paper trading simulator online and in light of current circumstances. In the game, you would be given $100,000 worth of virtual money, which you can invest in forex, options, and stocks among others. Thinkorswim additionally gives a cover of instructive webcasts. Thinkorswim PaperMoney is accessible for download. In case you're an accomplished client searching for an all the more energizing platform and are searching for more its advanced highlights, you will discover the value of utilizing Thinkorswim. Thinkorswim additionally has a dream stock market game.

Any trading simulator needs to combine realism with satisfaction. The simulators above are practical; in addition, a great deal of amusement to play on. However, to be an incredible piece of training innovation, a simulator needs to go past these fundamentals. I trust the rundown are compelling training tools in light of the fact that they were developed starting from the earliest stage with this as the main priority.

Now that you know it's possible to trade options without risking money, what are you sitting tight for? Register on these platforms and improve your options trading strategy today! Go on, trade without risking any money!

# Technical Analysis of Options

It's inescapable that the more you trade, the more you will feel a wide range of emotions. You'll experience all the full range of emotions, from the sadness of taking a loss to the bliss of closing a winning trade. You will question your life choices, and sometimes wonder why you ever decided to go into trading, and in other cases thinking you are in charge are destined to be a trader.

Greed and fear will be the two main feelings driving the choices you make. It doesn't make a difference whether you're making your hundredth trade or you're first. Greed and fear are inescapable.

Technical analysis works because everybody has to manage greed and fear, and it is something that can be found in the charts. Human habits don't change. You can trade technical analysis once you learn what they are.

To be successful as an options trader, you have to create and rely on strategies. Remember the time a move takes because options lose value over time. Comprehend the stats identified with options.

You want to make sure you can still see the chart whatever set of indicators you utilize. An excessive number of traders fill up their charts with so many lines and indicators that you can no longer see the price and volume. So you can concentrate on the data that genuinely matters, keep your charts clean. Add indicators that improve your insight, not cover it up. Just include the ones that will matter to your trading and keep all the others off your chart. Maintain your attention on price and volume.

# Chapter 4

# Specific Strategies for Trading Options

Stocks represent a unit of ownership that is issued by companies to the general public, allowing them to take possession of its assets and earnings. It is this claim to earnings that justifies earnings distribution to shareholders in the form of dividends. By simple calculation, an investor's claim to the assets of a company in which they hold shares increases as the percentage of their share ownership increases.

However, there are a few points about the finer details of stockholding that most people do not appreciate. First off, a stake in a company does not really equate to a stake in its assets. Your shares do not really make you a partial owner of the corporation you hold shares in because shares are issued by companies as more of a stake in their financial performance than the conventional kind of ownership. Corporations, being legally recognized persons, own their assets, file their own taxes, are sued and sue other legal entities and have the ability to take loans for their own expedient use.

So does owning the stocks of a company equate with the right to their assets? Not by a long shot. The principle of separation of rights and control governs the way shareholders interact with the assets of holding companies. With this principle, your share ownership is restricted to the amount of equity a company has offered to the public, not their assets, or even a portion of the company equivalent to the percentage of shares you own. This separation of shareholders' equity and the corporation itself is very important because it restricts liability for both. Even in the event of a bankruptcy, only the company's held assets may be sold. Your stake will remain as a nominal value of whatever value the stock market places on the company. In those adverse events, only the value of your shares will drop, but your ownership of them is not enforceable by any state body, which is to say that not even the courts can compel you to sell—you decide. For the corporation, its assets are protected from appropriation even by the shareholders who purportedly own a share of the business.

Even though shares do not constitute ownership rights in a business, they do equate to voting rights during shareholder meetings. The shareholder is also entitled to a share of the company's profits in dividends for those companies that reward its shareholders with them. The process of buying and selling shares is also simplified by the fact that there is no transference of asset ownership. Higher up in the share ownership hierarchy, shareholders also have enough voting power to be involved in seating the board of directors. In large corporations, the board of directors runs the company on behalf of the shareholders by appointing the senior managers, crafting the long-term strategy of the business and authorizing massive expenditures like acquisitions.

If stocks are not really a portion of the company a shareholder buys, and then what exactly are they? In many instances, companies issue stocks to the public to raise large amounts of money, distributing the capital risk to thousands (or millions) of people. Money raised in the initial public offering is then used to fund new business projects and propel it to greater heights. But raising capital is not the only reason why companies go public. Some companies, like software giant Microsoft, went public because of government regulations that require companies with a certain number of shareholders (over 500) to release their financial reports publicly. Rather than release financial reports like publicly traded companies but not enjoy the surplus of capital that comes with a public issue, companies like these opt to issue a portion of the business to the public. Another motivation for issuing the shares of a company to the public is to make it possible for employees to trade out their stakes in the company (usually offered as an incentive during employment) for real cash.

The stock market is the institution through which brokers and traders exchange their shares with other traders and brokers. A large number of them are involved in the stock trade whose liquidity of shares is quite high—there is always a willing buyer and a willing seller. Stock markets also facilitate the transfer of bonds and other securities. Only in the stock market can a shareholder hope to turn their stocks into liquid cash, especially because, as mentioned above, the assets of the company whose shares they hold are out of bounds.

There are two types of stocks issued by corporations—common and preferred.

## Comparison

What we have discussed above is essentially the common stock type of share ownership. Common stocks enable a person to hold a portion of a business but not take possession of it even though it gives them a limited right to influence the business operations of a company. On the other hand, preferred stocks, a hybrid share that is issued by a company for a very specific capital requirement, gives the holder zero say on a business's running—no voting rights, no right to influence the board of directors placement, and no consultation in the making of huge business decisions. For that reason, preferred stocks are little more like bonds than shares.

Investors with common stocks are entitled to a share of the company's profits in the form of dividends. These dividends are determined by the board of directors on a per-share basis. As for preferred stockholders, their claim to dividends is usually greater, taking precedence over common shareholders in terms of yield per share and priority. In the event of a company missing a dividend payout, preferred shareholders receive their arrears first. Preferred stockholder also takes precedence over common stockholders in the event of a company liquidating its operations. In fact, because of the greater claim of common stockholders to the business as owners (making decisions, voting, etc.), they are paid absolutely last behind holders of bonds, credit, and preferred shares.

The common stock is the most popular type of share for people to transact in. It performs much better than preferred shares in the stock market, but it is also more volatile. With a flexible interest rate, the return on capital invested in stock is determined solely by the perception of the stock market on the company's financial strength. The fixed interest rate of the preferred stock makes it less susceptible to market volatility in the stock market. Instead, their value is affected by interest rates of the general economy in an inverse manner. When the interest rates rise, the value of a preferred stock drops, and when it declines, their value climbs.

Another important distinction between common shares and preferred ones is the rights of the issuer to call them back. While common stocks may only be bought back in the event of a company going bankrupt or folding, preferred stocks may be repurchased at a prefixed time or any time the company decides to call them back. The company then pays shareholders a redemption rate to investors, often a higher rate of return than expected. One of the factors that affect the price of preferred stocks is actually the anticipation of a callback. The sooner a company is likely to call back preferred shares issued to the public, the more in demand those shares become as investors seek to capitalize on the premium redemption rate.

## Stock Issuance: The IPO Process

The initial public offering (IPO) is the process through which a company issues shares to the public. An IPO represents the blowing wide open of the shareholder register, previously dominated by founders, early and angel investors and employees (in those companies where the stock option is an incentive for attracting and retaining employees) to include as many of the public as the number of shares a company offers. The price of a company's stock, especially shortly after the IPO, is determined in part by its book value and the number of people who are willing to buy its shares at a certain price. The higher the demand, the higher the stock price climbs. As a prospective investor in the stock market, it is only natural that you are fascinated by the whole IPO process. After all, the understanding of what goes on behind the scenes of an IPO often determines whether an investor considers the freshly issued shares worth buying or not.

There are several ways for a company to go public, but the Securities and Exchange Commission (SEC), a government department mandated with overseeing the stock market and enforcing fair play rules, follows each and every one of them very closely. The most popular format of public issuance is one where an investment bank spearheads the process. In fact, this format is so popular that it is referred to in most literature as the legitimate definition of an IPO.

However, there are other alternative procedures for a company to follow in issuing their shares to the public. They are direct listing and Dutch action.

## Investment Bank

A bank-issued initial public offering is a five-step journey from private holding to public trading that is overseen by an investment bank from start to finish. First, the business leaders in a company decide to go public, with the intention of raising money or simply in compliance with government regulations.

However, because the offering process is a complicated and tightly regulated process, having a firm that specializes in the stock market can be a very good idea.

## Selecting the Bank

The first thing to do in the IPO process is to select a bank to underwrite the whole process. By underwriting, we mean that the bank buys or commits to buying in principle all the shares a company intends to issue to the public and then re-issue them in the secondary stock market.

This is an important role for a bank to play in such a key process of a company's financial maturity, so some due diligence is very much in order. Usually, what a business looks for in an underwriter is reputation. Investment banks, like Goldman Sachs, have taken many iconic companies public because their ranking, as some of the best investment firms on Wall Street, gives them a certain appeal to wary executives. An investment bank with a specialty in a business's line of operation gives it an edge because it is perceived as having a better grasp of the institutional investors who might be brought on board during the IPO.

Talking of institutional investors, they are very critical to the success of an initial public offering for a few reasons. But to understand that better, let us first jump slightly ahead and consider the landscape immediately after a company goes public. A spike in the price is usually expected soon after the IPO. This is the most effective way to create a stable foundation for a company's shares to take off and increase in value over time. To do this, some companies offer their shares to the public at a point where confidence in their future financial performance is high. The SEC enforces a period of lockdown, where transactions are restricted. This quiet period ensures that market hype does not drive the share price too far above its real value and exacerbate the volatility of the whole stock market. When employees and initial investors start selling to take advantage of the short-term rise in price, the share price often drops drastically because of oversupply. Institutional investors, on the other hand, invest for the long haul. They are unlikely to engage in this kind of maneuverings, which makes the stock more stable. This makes it more important for a business to select an investment bank that can rope in the big fish to increase hype and subscription rates.

## Due Diligence

The next process in the investment bank format of IPOs is the performance of due diligence checks and conducting the regulatory filings. As mentioned above, the investment bank assumes the responsibility of getting all the shares a company intends to sell to the public and resells it, acting as the middleman between it and the investors. There are various arrangements that the company can enter with the investment bank on the process.

A firm commitment entails a bank undertaking to buy all the shares and re-issue them to the general public. For an investment bank to agree to this arrangement, it has to be very confident that it will be able to make money on the IPO from the underwriting fees and mark-up of selling at a higher price than what they buy the shares for.

Another strategy is called the best effort agreement, whereby the underwriter speculates the amount of money they anticipate to raise from the IPO. Because there is no assurance that the target will be hit, the bank does not undertake to buy all the shares. Its job is simply to issue the stocks to the public for the company. Nonetheless, the bank is expected to promote the shares to the public and institutional investors.

For IPOs that are too big for one underwriter to handle alone, a syndicate is created, with each member contributing to the pool of money required to purchase the whole issue in full from the issuing company. The bank that raises the largest share takes the lead on the offering, keeping the books and overseeing the more crucial aspects of the IPO for a greater share of the underwriting fees. This way, an investment bank distributes the risk of the IPO to a large group of competing banks.

In fact, this is the most intricate process of the offering. Important documents are crafted, SEC requirements have to be followed, and some very delicate accounting mathematics has to be done, often with a contracted accounting firm for impartiality. A reimbursement clause protects the investment bank from losses in the event of the issuing company withdrawing the offer midway through the process by stipulating that the expenses are to be reimbursed either way. In a letter of intent, the underwriter commits to the offering process by promising to dedicate every effort to ensure that the shares will perform well in the stock market, including promoting to investment bankers among other promotional efforts. On its part, the issuing company commits to provide all information needed by the underwriter and to cooperate in the whole issuance process.

Other important documents in the due diligence process include the registration statement, which is submitted to the SEC showing the financials, management background, ticker symbol suggested for use in the stock markets, holdings by company insiders, and the legal history of a company. The registration statement filed with the SEC identifies the issued company as a component of the stock market and allows the SEC to keep tabs on their financial, legal, and accounting practices.

A prospectus is drafted for all investors, showing the strengths and weaknesses of a company, as a way of giving every prospective investor sufficient and reliable information about the impending share issue. From the prospectus, investors can speculate on the future of the company and make a better decision of whether to participate in the IPO. Another item created for the investors is the red herring document, which is used during the promotional roadshows where the underwriters and issuers promote the impending share issue to the public. The roadshows allow both the bank and the issuing company to gauge interest and demand for the impending share issue, which is important for the next part of the process—pricing.

## Stock Pricing

After evaluating the prospectus and verifying that all records are in order, the SEC gives approval for the IPO. The issue date is decided between the SEC, the issuing company, and the investment bank underwriting the process. And on the eve of the effective offering, the issuer and the investment bank sit to decide on the best price for the shares. Haggling on share price often comes down to a few cents per share. With millions of shares and billions in net worth often being the stake, every cent counts.

The price set for the stock during this seating depends on a few factors. The most important of these is the subscription rate for the share. During the roadshows, pre-orders are recorded in the order books. Shares that have been oversubscribed are preferred because this indicates greater confidence in the company's future by the stock market. Another consideration is the price at which the issuing company intended to sell its shares in the first place. In order to decide this, the share price for companies in the same industry is assessed. The issuer may want to have their shares sell at a higher or a lower price.

The stock price is calculated against the amount of money expected to be raised to determine the price of each share. The money a company expects to raise and the share of the company to be issued dictate the number of shares and value of each share on the negotiating table. But in the market, after trading opens up, all that matters is market hype, because this determines the enthusiasm of the market and, subsequently, the prices to which the share rises immediately after the IPO.

## Trading

The first day a company trades in the stock market is usually very exciting. Depending on the levels of excitement exhibited by buyers, the price either falls higher or lower to the one that the issuer agreed to with their investment bank. The trend established on the first day in terms of volumes traded and price trend may continue for a while, but restrictions placed by the SEC on trading soon after the IPO somewhat limit the volumes of transactions. As such, it is not until a few months after the initial offering that a stock stabilizes.

## The Stabilization Process

The undertaker does not disengage from the sharing process immediately after the stocks start trading publicly. They stick around to provide the market with analysis and expert commentary to boost demand. Other mitigating actions to maintain the stock price at the desired price include batch buying or selling to influence the direction of the price shifts that take place soon after the IPO. During this time, the SEC restrictions on price manipulation are usually suspended to allow the stock to pick up at a price that is more realistic.

Incidentally, it is for this exact reason that it is ill-advised to buy into a company soon after its IPO. The price, immediately after the initial offering, is usually artificially modified, which makes it unpredictable afterward when the laws of demand and supply finally take over.

While complicated, the process of issuing shares through an investment bank presents the issuer with greater control over investor interest and stock price after the IPO. The expert guidance of the investment with the SEC regulations that come with initial public offerings also goes a long way in smoothing the process out. The main disadvantage of using an investment bank is that they charge quite an exorbitant underwriting fee and also make a ton of money on the mark-up between the price agreed with the issuer and what the public ends up paying for the shares. Perhaps it is for these reasons that some companies decide to go directly to the public.

## Direct Listing

By listing the company's shares on the stock exchange at the same time that they are offered for purchase by the public, a company skips the process of hunting and negotiating with a bank to take the company public. The company also saves on underwriting fees and enjoys all the sweetness of an oversubscribed stock with a price higher than the book value. However, a company that opts for a direct listing forfeits the advantages of having an experienced Wall Street firm promoting the IPO. The stock price from a stock that has been listed directly starts off rather sluggishly.

The companies that are well suited for direct listings are those that are considerably well known already, offering a product that the public is already well aware of. Even if the institutional investors may not join the fray earlier on, the market buzz for its products more than makes up for the lack of an investment banker. Moreover, when investors show more genuine interest in the stock, the price grows organically, driven by real demand rather than blatant price manipulation. One of the most recent direct listings was the 2018 Spotify Technology SA.

## Dutch Auction

A Dutch auction allows the buyers to set their own price for a share. A company approaches investors and requests for the number of shares they would like to buy of their company and their price of those shares, relying on the market perception of the business's financial well-being to set a reasonable price. The highest bid price almost always wins the auction and sets the price of a company's shares. Dutch auctions rely on connections to spread the word and give investors the chance to buy shares.

One of the most iconic Dutch auctions of the twenty-first century is that of Alphabet Inc., Google's parent company. Some other companies like Morningstar Inc. and the Boston Beer Company, Inc. have also helped Dutch auctions, issuing their shares to a selected group of people.

## Why Invest in the Stock Market?

There are many reasons why investors, both professional and beginners, choose the stock market as their preferred vehicle for investment. The main reason why people do so, however, are those stocks having a better interest rate than most other investments? Unlike a savings account, money devoted to the stock market makes returns way above the inflation rate—as long as the investing has been done with a bit of skill.

## Investment Value

Over the long term, stocks have the highest rate of returns when compared to other asset classes. For example, the Standard & Poor 500 Index (S&P 500) had an average annual interest rate of about 11% from 1928 to 2016. To put this in perspective, the Rule of 72 is used to determine how long it would take for an investment to double in value at a certain rate of return (RoR) by dividing the RoR with the number 72. With 11%, the time frame falls somewhere between six and a half years and seven years. For other investments like treasury bills that have an estimated annual rate of return of 3.46%, the time it takes to double the investment comes in at slightly over 20 years! That is a long time difference between two asset classes that are both traded in the same stock market.

## Return on Investment for Stocks versus Short-Term Bonds

Investments are evaluated by the value for money that they generate for the investor above and beyond the inflation rate.

Whatever the rate of inflation in a given year, it should be factored into the calculations when considering true returns. The higher the rate of return, the better the gain on capital will be even with inflation being high. The stock market, therefore, presents all investors with value for their money in the form of greater rewards, a variety of investments that one can put their money into, like mutual funds, index funds, ETFs, international indexes, etc. Finally, the fees are considerably lower if you decide to go for discount brokers. More pricey stockbrokers also offer some investing advice, which is a surefire way to increase potential returns.

## Dividends

A dividend is the share of a company's annual earnings that is shared out with the investors, with every share allocated a fixed payout depending on how much the company made that year. Dividends are viewed by most investors as free money because they add to your already appreciating initial investment whose value is dictated by the market forces in the stock market. For example, if you buy the stocks of company X for $50 and one year later they have risen to $56, then that is an average rate of return of about 12%. However, if the company also issued a dividend payout of 3% on every share, then that is an extra 3% in returns that your investment just produced for you in that year. It is so great because a dividend is money you get on top of the nominal rate of return for your stock investment—free money, so to say.

The dividend is paid out in various forms, but the most prominent buyback and cash reward are the most common. In the cash reward option, the company credits every investor's account with a sum of money equivalent to the number of shares they hold with the company multiplied by the dividend payout rate. If the investor wants to reinvest this extra money back into the company, they can do so at their discretion. The buyback option is where a company offers investors with a dividend reinvestment plan to use their dividends to buy more shares at better terms.

The announcement date is the date on which a company discloses to the public that they intend to pay a certain amount of money to every shareholder. This payout is approved by the shareholders, so announcement dates usually come after the annual general meeting. The record date is the latest time an investor has to have bought the share for them to be eligible for the dividend. After a certain time, the ex-dividend date, shareholders are ineligible for dividends because they bought after the company had already settled on a certain rate based on the existing shareholder register. And of course, the payment date is the time at which the dividend payout is actually injected into the accounts of the shareholders.

# Bonds

Bonds have been in existence since time immemorial. They were used by ancient governments to raise money for various capital-intensive causes, which is the same used to which they are put even today. So what exactly are bonds? In the stock trading sense of the word, a bond is like a unit of a bigger loan that a company or government takes from a large pool of investors for a specific purpose. The whole loan, thus taken, also falls under the definition of a bond. What individual investors hold in their hands as the bond is usually the certificate given to signify the borrower/lender relationship they enter into with the borrower. In the bond certificate, the terms of payment and details of the loan are indicated, including the interest rate and maturity date. Trading in bonds can either be over the counter in the bourse or between lender and borrower.

# How Bonds Work

The system of bond borrowing can be traced way back to the ancient Mesopotamian financial systems, where corporations borrowed grain with the promise to pay back the principal plus interest at a certain date. Instead of placing the company assets as surety, a bond was used instead, symbolizing the borrower's deepest commitment to repay the loan. This obligation to repay the debt became to represent the bond the current world knows as financial systems evolved. Bonds are necessitated by a number of realities that only the insider might know about the capital markets.

The capital requirements of large corporations are quite extensive. To start a new project, finance ongoing operations (especially in R & D), and repay old debts that have not been repaid yet, companies need to raise massive amounts of money. From large infrastructural projects to war efforts, governments have an appetite for capital that is tax remissions from citizens and businesses do not meet.

In some cases, the banks cannot meet the demand for these needs simply because the amount of money these entities require is so great. The risk of a bank going under in the event of these massive borrowers defaulting is too great, which means that corporations and governments have to become creative about how they raise the money for whatever their super-important need might be.

The way to do this is by distributing the risk to so many people that the effect of a possible default is blunted by the very fact that it is spread over many people. Having 10,000 people risk $1,000 each is preferable to one entity risking the $10,000,000 because the impact would be less serious on each person. With a single lender, such a huge default would definitely take the lender under.

Bonds are considered to be quite conservative as investment options, mostly because the possibility of losing one's money is way low. Short of going out of business, bond issuers repay their debt obligations in full, and even in the event of going bankrupt, bonds are treated as creditors and paid first from the liquefied assets of a company. Governments absolutely pay their bonds, sometimes issuing a new bond just to repay the old.

## Characteristics of Bonds

While there are quite a number of types of bonds, some of their characteristics are uniform to them all. Understanding the characteristics and terminologies used to describe them is crucial to learning how to invest in them.

The face value is the principal amount that the issuer is expected to pay the holder of a bond when the period that has been agreed upon passes. The face value remains fixed over time even when the supply and demand drive the price up in the stock market. These external influences of the stock market determine whether the bond sells at a premium (higher than the face value) or a discount (lower than the price indicated on the bond certificate).

The maturity, of course, is the due date for the bond's principal. The issuer decides the maturity period for the bond, and the market responds by buying into the idea with their money. A lengthy maturity time increases the risk of nonpayment, so the issuer has to promise a higher yield to entice investors.

At the time of issuing the bond, the borrower promises to pay a certain amount over the face value, which is otherwise known as the interest rate or the yield/coupon. The coupon is the equivalent of servicing a loan, with the borrower expected to pay a certain amount every year or semi-annually. This coupon could be fixed (which means that it never changes despite the state of the economy), or it could be adjustable, allowing the borrower to vary their coupon payment depending on certain market conditions.

Because their interest rates are either fixed or more rigid than the rest of the stock market, bonds are considered to be a safe haven for conservative investors during an economic crisis. Lower interest rates in the general economy drive the interest of a bond higher due to increased demand. The increased demand comes about because investors suddenly view bonds as being more profitable even if their price remains the same. Bond yield thus moves in an inverse direction with interest rates in the rest of the market—down when the former is high and high when it is low. Another factor that affects yield is the rate of inflation. With their low-interest rates, bonds become attractive when the inflation rate is lower because the net yield increases. Short-term bonds that are expected to be exposed to a shorter period of inflation tend to have a lower interest rate while those with a longer maturity period (and thus risk) require a greater interest in recompense.

Based on the yield, we have several types of bonds. The common one is the coupon bond where the issuer pays a certain amount of money above the face value of a bond. Another type of bond is the zero-coupon type, which is issued at a discounted rate compared to the face value. When the bond matures, the bond is paid in full, and the investor makes their money that way. The United States treasury bills are traded as zero-coupon bonds, so a $100 note sells at, say, $98. At maturity, the inflation-adjusted interest rate will be around 2.5%.

Another type of bond is the convertible type. This one allows bondholders to take the decision to convert their bond principal and use it to buy stocks. The option to convert debt into equity when the share price reaches a certain level allows private bond issuers to reduce the coupon. The lowered interest rate at the point of issuance serves the company better as the project takes off, and the fact that the debt is converted into equity dilutes the stakes of other shareholders at no cost to the company. As for the investors, the convertible bond presents double insurance for their investment. If the share does not reach levels attractive for purchasing, the bond yield is still high enough to give a considerably good return. But the fact that they can convert the bond into stock at any time, at any stock price, means that the investor gets their pick of the best moments to buy shares, which could be very profitable.

A similar but somewhat different type of bond is the callable type that may be redeemed by the issuer at any point before the maturity. The callable bond allows the issuer to buy back the debt at lower interest rates and re-issue at a cheaper cost. Because issuers buy the bonds back when interest rates are in decline, it means that the bondholders are relieved of their bonds at just the point when the price is in an upward trajectory. For that reason, investors do not overly like callable bonds and opt for non-callable types when the coupon rate, maturity, and credit rating of the company is the same.

## Bonds Issuers

The three main types of entities issue bonds are corporate, municipals, and governments. The government is the main bond issuer, responsible for more than 50% of all bonds floating around in the stock market. The treasury issues bonds on behalf of the government, with the word assigned to them varying by their maturity rate. Bonds that are expected to mature within the year are defined as bills, those that mature within ten years of being issued are known as notes, and those that are expected to mature ten to twenty years after their issue are known simply as bonds. The more conventional name for all three categories of government-issued bonds is treasuries. It is not uncommon to hear them all being referred to as treasury bills, treasury notes, and treasury bonds respectively.

Local governments issue bonds to raise money for certain development projects. Because these bonds are unfamiliar and investors are often unsure whether the issuer can actually pay up, the coupon income is often specified as being tax-free in a bid to attract more investors.

## Comparison with Stocks

The main difference between bonds and stocks is that stocks represent a stake in the business while a bond is essentially a credit service an investor extends to the company or the government. The only reason corporate entities and governments issue bonds is to raise money while stocks may also be issued to comply with government regulations. While the money raised during an IPO goes a long way to boost the company's operations, it is often held as liquid assets because an IPO is simply a matter of a business going public to increase its legitimacy and boost public confidence in its products. An initial public offering is a statement that a company is past the start-upstage. A bond issue means nothing more than that a company needs money for operations and wishes to borrow.

Another area where stocks and bonds differ is in maturity. While bonds come with a pre-arranged maturity date, stocks are perpetual. One can hold on to a stock for as long as they wish, collecting dividends on their investment for as long as a whole century. The longest maturity time for a bond is about 30–50 years.

The way that investors make money from either a stock or a bond also differs. With a stock, the price appreciates over time, raising the purported value of an investment (the money a person would make if they sold their shares at this exact moment). This rise is determined by the laws of demand and supply, such that when the market perceives the company as being healthy financially, the price rises because there is greater demand. The opposite is true when the company is struggling financially and enjoys no confidence in the stock market.

From an investment perspective, stocks and bonds differ in one key area, and that is the perception of security for them both. A stock is viewed as a volatile investment because its price is likely to drop at any time. Even though the overall interest rate of publicly traded companies maintains the lower double digits levels, some perform very badly and often go into the negative for protracted periods of time. This volatility makes it extremely hard to predict the return that an investment will bring. For a bond, the interest rate is predetermined and mostly fixed, save for slight deviations up and down, depending on the state of the economy and interest rates. A bond is considered to be safe and conservative, bringing a stabilizing effect to an investment portfolio. Stocks, on the other hand, come with high risk and high reward and tend to make a portfolio substantially more unpredictable.

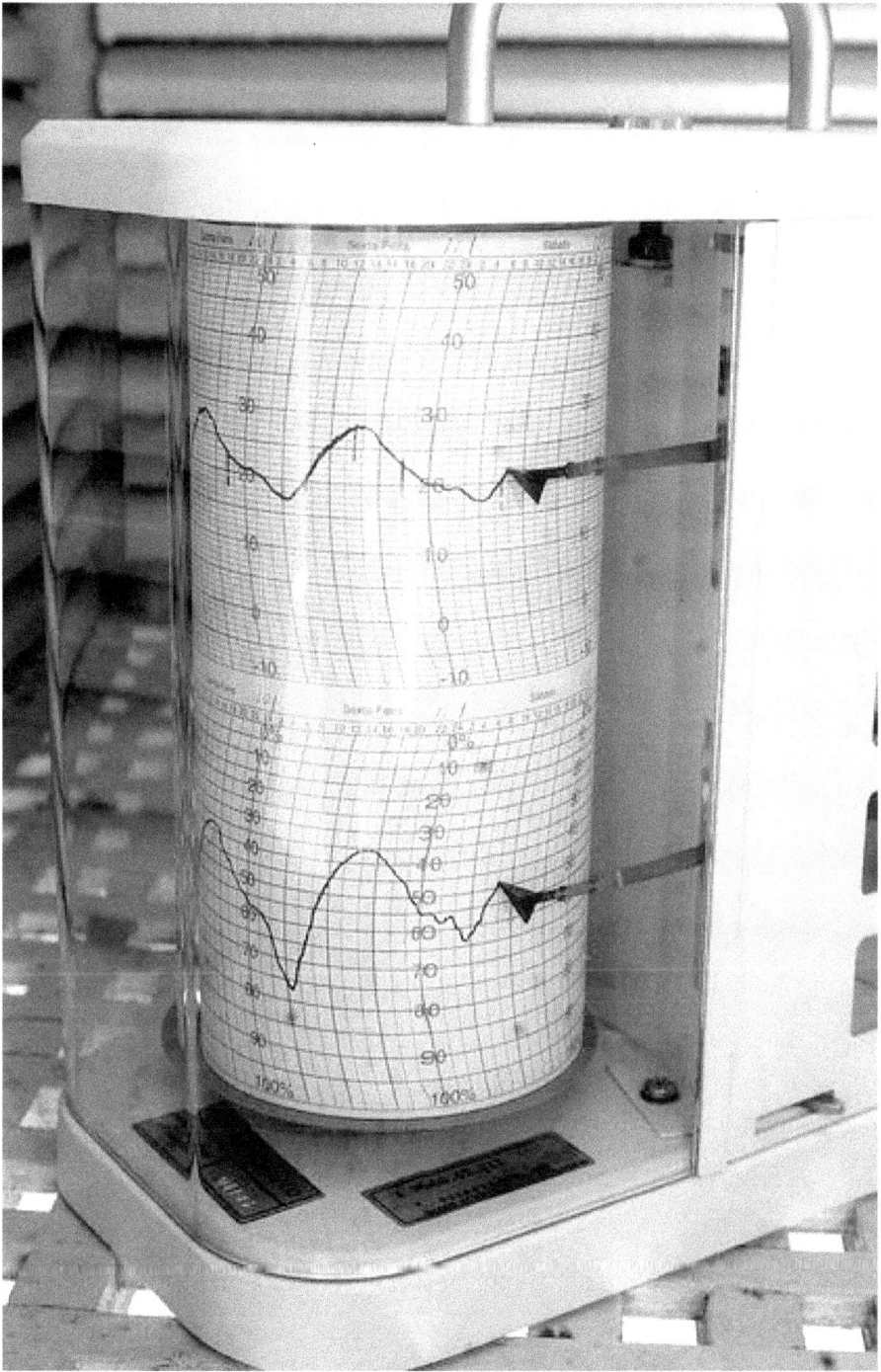

# Chapter 5

# Risk Measurement

## The Necessary Phase of Learning

The first phase in trading is to know your environment well and to master the tools that will be mobilized. The number of people rushing into the markets without controlling anything is simply staggering.

Before being able to conquer the markets, the trader must first master the rules of the game. He must know the stakeholders, the tools for decision-making, and the analysis methods that work best in his market (technical and technical analysis). / or fundamental analysis), well-mastering money management and risk management. This is an often exciting phase as the trader discovers a new field and tries to learn as much as possible. Enthusiasts will read all books available on the domain subscribe to stock market letters, attend seminars and whatnot.

At Jack Schwager's question, how did you learn to trade, Baldwin responds, "I started one lot at a time. I always had an opinion. All-day I stayed on the floor and I developed an opinion. When I saw that my opinion was working, I was reinforced in my approach even if I did not trade. I realized that by standing six hours a day, every day, most of the time I was right. I saw the same scenarios to develop recurrently. Some market patterns were repeated and market operators would make the same mistakes day after day. You just had to grab them."

This market initiation phase, therefore, should not be overlooked and is a prerequisite. Nevertheless, during this period novice traders will seek techniques to achieve a significant performance while the most important for a beginner is primarily to train and manage its risk to be ready when the time comes. The trader must learn to walk before running: the money management saves time to learn the ropes.

## Risk Management: An Imperative

Good risk Management enables the trader to ensure his survival and therefore to retain his most valuable work tool, namely his capital. A ruined trader no longer has the opportunity to exercise his activity. In addition, risk management allows it to focus primarily on the best opportunities. Indeed, there are multiple opportunities in the markets but the trader must first select those that offer the lowest risk for a high potential of gain.

A trader who manages his risk correctly controls the probabilities. Indeed, the biggest danger in trading is to think you have found the magic formula because it is easy to be intoxicated by success and to believe yourself infallible. If you follow Sun Tzu, a person who thinks he is infallible becomes extremely vulnerable. Therefore, the trader must manage his risk even more strictly after a series of winnings. Unfortunately, this situation often corresponds to a euphoric state of the trader who begins to have disproportionate confidence in his "instinct" and ends up making dramatic mistakes.

## Larry Hite Risk Management

For the best traders, it is important to respect the risk. The famous trader Larry Hite even considers respect for risk as one of the creeds of his hedge fund. According to him, before making money, the job of the trader is not to lose. L. Hite strictly controls his risk and applies these principles:

His system never positions itself against the dominant tendency. There is no exception and he always follows his system; the maximum risk on each position is limited to 1% of its total capital;

Diversification is taken seriously; volatility is monitored in each market to generate signals to liquidate or suspend trading in a market.

Always follow the trend and we never deviate from the method. The positions are all the same. There are bad bets and good bets. Many people think that a losing trade is a bad bet. That's wrong; you can lose money even on a good bet. If the probability of success is 50% and you expect a gain of two dollars for a dollar risk, then it is a good bet even if you lose

## The Art of Achieving One's Goals without Taking Risks

Contrary to a widespread belief, the best traders take a very little risk. They put risk management at the top of their trading plan. Performance is only the result of strict monitoring of the plan. When the title evolves against its original scenario, the trader must seek to get out of his position as soon as possible. He can, of course, wait for a rebound to come out with a lesser loss, but he must never drag on and go into hope mode.

Linda Bradford Raschke explains the importance of testing the markets: "In trading, part of the process involves testing the markets. If the timing of your entry is good enough, you will not lose much even when you are wrong."

In trading, you have to manage your risk and the profits will come naturally, the art of lasting is it not the key to success? The trader must identify situations where the risk is low (close stop)

and the potential for high gain. He will have to avoid situations where the risk is too high even if the potential is interesting and wait only for the best opportunities.

One must always think about the consequences of one's actions. The ruin is the financial death of the trader. Indeed, it is difficult in this case to go back and rebuild its capital. The trader must above all aim for survival even when he is at the top of his game. Indeed, it is often at this moment that it is the most fragile.

## Sometimes Escape Is the Best Alternative

According to Paul Tudor Jones, "we must always favor defense to attack". If we have a losing position that places us in an uncomfortable situation, there is a simple rule: to get out of his position at any cost in order to regain his senses and wait for a new interesting entry point. It is always possible to come back, ˉ and a trader must convince himself that there is nothing better than a fresh start.

Bruce Kovner evokes the importance he gives to his stops, (a level that invalidates our scenario and must trigger an exit from our position): "Every time I open a position I have a predetermined stop. This is the only way for me to sleep. I know where I'm going before I get home. I always place my stop over a technical barrier. A technical barrier is a level that the market should not touch if our scenario is good. I organized my life so that my stops are followed religiously."

During doubtful phases, the trader should stay out of the markets. It is useless to position ourselves if the probabilities are not favorable to us. You do not have to be in the market all the time. This exhibition is vain and useless. The leak can be beneficial in trading. It is even, for P. Fayard, "the stratagem of the stratagems". Indeed, when a conflict cannot find a favorable outcome, the best choice is the leak because it means that the trader preserves his capital for better times, which will not fail to occur.

To summarize, the trader will have to survive on the markets first and foremost. Profits are only the natural result of the application of his "survival" plan.

## Know-How to Attack

As discussed in the section devoted to psychological analysis, when the dominant consensus is not confirmed by stock market movements, the market is probably turning around. This is a period when the convention dominant changes occur, and a trader who detects these changes can advantageously position itself. The trader must strive to wait for the best moment before positioning himself. Opportunities will come to him and will result from mistakes made by other competitors. Thus, the trader is essentially concerned with his defense and does not hesitate to seize opportunities as soon as they occur.

But a good defense should not mean inertia. Indeed, sometimes the best defense is the attack and if the general does not dare to attack, the enemy will update his fear and use it at his expense.

## The Psychological Problems That Arise When Opening a Position

The trader can encounter various psychological problems when opening a position: Decision made without real reflection: a trader is primarily a man subject to cognitive and emotional bias. Thus, a trader who identifies a familiar configuration that has earned him money in the past will base his decision on this information alone to position. He falsely conceals all the other data, whereas he should above all aim for perfect rationality, to act.

Impulsiveness: The trader is afraid of missing the opportunity of the century and rushes forgetting the rules set out in his trading plan. If the trader receives a signal but for one reason or another he misses the entry, he will have to wait for another favorable entry point before positioning himself. Rushing hastily on a title is a dangerous act. Often, certain emotions such as euphoria, the fear of missing a movement are at the origin of the rush of the trader and incite him to make decisions not thoughtful.

Inertia: the trader sees an opportunity but does nothing to seize it. The trader must dare to seize the opportunities that arise if he wants to achieve a positive and above all sustainable performance. The trader may wish to wait for other items that confirm his point of view. The information is never perfect but by doing this, the trader will position itself at a time when all the operators have already perceived this information and are therefore already positioned. The growth potential of the asset will be limited. The trader must, therefore, dare to enter at the very beginning of a movement if enough elements are going in this direction.

The rationality of traders is limited in the sense of Simon: instead of performing a thorough analysis, the trader will take into account one or two factors and neglect others. This low-quality analysis is of little use in the decision-making process. A good trader should not overlook any parameters before making his decision. All contingencies must be taken into account by the trader who must aim for perfect rationality even if this is impossible in fact. Indeed, it must base its decision on relevant and complete information. Nevertheless, markets are governed by uncertainty and the trader will never be able to obtain perfect information. He will have to be content with solid information putting the probabilities in his camp and make his decision knowingly, that is to say by not neglecting the risk and placing a stop.

## Attack When the Probabilities Are Favorable To Us

The object of the battle is to win the victory and not to satisfy his desire for revenge. The trader must not open a position in vain, and he must enter a title only if the potential advantage is much higher than the tolerated loss. The great traders are like the great generals: they do not engage if they are not convinced that victory is within their reach; they know how to save the strength of their troops and go on the offensive only if the interest is real.

## Applying the Risk / Reward Concept to Elliott Waves

The waves are used to define risk zones and therefore stop levels. They are also used by operators to determine targets. In this section, we will use Elliott's Fibonacci ratios and waves and show how these tools can be useful in determining the Risk / Reward ratio.

# Anticipation of a Wave 3

Playing a wave 3 is always very interesting in terms of Risk / Reward. Wave 3 is often a powerful wave with high potential and limited risk. In addition, we have seen in the chart analysis section that the standard retracement ratio of Wave 1 is 61.8%. In other words, wave 2, which corrects wave 1, will often trace 61.8% of the movement and sometimes even (in extreme cases) 100% of the movement.

After studying the market, if a trader believes that a stock is about to draw a bullish acceleration in wave 3, he may initiate a position on the retracement ratio at 50% Wave 1 and strengthen its position on the next ratio to 61.8%. From this perspective, it will be able to place a stop under the ratio at 76.4% or even under the 100% retracement, under the old low point.

The same reasoning can be applied to type 4 corrective waves. The standard retracement ratio of a wave 4 is 38.2% and it is possible for a trader to position himself around this level and place a stop under the ratio of 50% to play the impulsive wave named 5.

# Can We Determine The Optimal Size Of A Position?

We will seek to determine the share of capital that can be risky for a known probability of success and a payoff ratio. Stops are an important part of risk management, but they are just one aspect of money management. Money management, which focuses on the size of the position and not on the right timing, seeks to answer the question: what is the optimal size of the position?

We will attempt to answer this question by first examining a basic system that relies on a uniform risk for each position, and then we will elaborate on this approach using Kelly's formula.

## Uniform Risk per Trade

This approach recommends risking an identical amount for all positions initiated. The main advantage of this strategy is its simplicity even if it lacks flexibility. Thus, for each position initiated, the trader will risk an amount of € 1,000 for example. The main problem with this approach is that this amount may be too large if the trader suffers several successive losses, or too low if the trader records several successive gains. Many traders prefer the approach that risks a fixed percentage of capital.

# Fixed Share of Risk Capital

With this system, the trader limits his risk to a fixed proportion of the capital available to him. Thus, if the capital decreases, the risk will decrease proportionally. Similarly, if capital increases, because of realized gains, the tolerable risk per position will increase. The trader has a capital of one million euros and the fixed portion of the capital at risk is 1% per position. The risk tolerated by open position will, therefore, be € 10,000.

# Kelly's Formula

Many traders have relied on Kelly's formula (scientist working for Bell) to determine the optimal size of the position.

$K\% = W - ((1 - W) / R)$

- With K% = percentage of capital that can be risky on a position;
- W = probability of success of the system;
- R = historical payoff ratio.

This formula indicates that the optimal portion that can be risky will increase with the payoff ratio and the probability of success. The trader cannot change market conditions and therefore will have no influence on his probability of success or his payoff ratio. The only parameter he can modify and that he is able to control thanks to money management is the size of his position.

# Criticisms of Kelly's Formula

To criticize this formula, we will base ourselves on the people who exercise a day trading activity. Often, the probability of success is high, and the payoff ratio is equal to unity. Good day traders and scalpers often have a 70% probability of success and a payoff ratio of 1. Based on Kelly's formula, optimal exposure of Kelly should be 40%. But this figure leaves us perplexed: it means that if the trader loses three times in a row he is ruined.

The trader must for its tranquility reduce the risk taken for each position so that even losing several times in a row (let's take a series of 20 losses for example) it is not ruined. We even think that the rules must be even stricter than this: a day trader who loses 5/10% of his capital in one day must stop all activity and then return the next day fresh and available.

# Patience Is the Key

"Trading is very much like surfing. I try to take a wave or good time and if unfortunately, I miss it, I'm waiting for the next."

As explained Weinstein, like the cheetah, the trader must wait to be responsive to the real opportunities. The cheetah, though it is the fastest animal in the world, will wait to be absolutely sure to catch its prey before attacking. He can hide for a week, waiting for the right moment. The trader must always be extremely defensive and attack only when conditions are favorable. He cannot force the market to draw his favorite storyline and must simply bend to his will and wait for a perfect opportunity. He must then ask himself before the opening of his position: "Does this position deserve to be taken? Wouldn't it be better to wait for another opportunity? Patience is, therefore, the watchword for the army general as well as for the trader."

Formerly those who were experienced in the art of combat made themselves invincible, waited for the enemy to be vulnerable, and never engaged in wars that they foresaw not having to finish with advantage. Before undertaking them, they were sure of success. If the opportunity to go against the enemy was not favorable, they waited for happier times.

Thus, the trader can be defeated only by his own fault, and he can only be victorious through the fault of his enemies. Great traders know that there are times when you have to let others work for you. Novice traders do all the work and allow professionals to seize low-risk opportunities. It is important for the trader to be able to return at the right time and retire quickly when market conditions demand. According to Linda Bradford Rashke, it is important to enter the markets around the best possible levels.

She considers that timing is crucial because it buys time and allows seeing how the market will react.

## Stay In Control in All Circumstances at All Times

For trader Marc Ritchie, the strategy is to capitalize on the panic of other operators: "A trader must be able to think clearly and act decisively when other operators panic. The irrational markets are those on which we find the best opportunities. Traditionally, in a volatile market, even veteran traders prefer to stay out of business while this situation represents an opportunity to make money. As the saying goes, if you can keep your cool when others lose their heads then you can make a fortune. The trader is able to position himself against the majority opinion. The good trader remains true to his ideas and closes his ears to interpretations of the crowd that does not take the same positions. You have to have the courage to face the crowd, make a decision and execute it. The ability to think clearly and to have the courage to make a decision when others panic is an indispensable element for the trader. This is possible by having a trading plan. I mentally prepare for the market by developing several strategies in advance and plan what I plan to do if the X or Y scenario occurs."

A good trader knows when to be defensive (unclear market potential of trade already achieved, etc.). If the trader is positioned to buy and the market still seems powerful to him, instead of taking his profits, he will probably have to increase his position in order to take advantage of the amplitude of the current movement.

A good trader is able to determine when it is wise to defend and when to attack. A good strategist does not hesitate to implement his strategy when he is convinced of his solidity. He took care to analyze everything and took into account the different elements.

The good strategist has another quality which is the ability to change strategy if he thinks he has gone astray or if something is missing in his diagnosis. He will not hesitate in this case to modify his plans if the conditions require it. The wars in Iraq or Vietnam are classic cases where the military (in this case the US President) has stubbornly stuck instead of adapting its strategy to the context.

## Play the Probabilities

Never engage in small actions that you are sure they will turn to your advantage, and still, do not do it if you are not forced to, but above all be careful to commit to a general action if you are not assured of a complete victory. It is very dangerous to have precipitation in similar cases; a risky, ill-timed battle can completely ruin you: the least that can happen to you, if the event is doubtful, or you only half succeed, is to see you frustrated by the greater part of your hopes, and not being able to reach your ends.

## Behind Every Position, There Must Always Be a Reason

The trader must avoid at all costs the positions taken in uncalculated anticipation and with the sole motive to occupy his time because they can have extremely negative and damaging consequences. On the markets, the trader is not remunerated by the number of trades and his performance will depend closely on the success of his trading system as well as the average gain-to-loss ratio. Any position must be open only based on specific criteria respecting the trading plan.

## Stay Away From Markets When Conditions Are Not Optimal

In extremely volatile markets, there is sometimes no logic and opportunities are few or difficult to grasp. Some traders are desperate and operate in a totally irrational way, which gives rise to movements on which the trader will struggle to capitalize.

After the publication of a large economic figure, the trader has every interest in waiting for the markets to calm down before settling. Indeed, stock prices are often erratic and the probability of anticipating a movement is minimal. The trader must avoid situations where the probabilities are not favorable to him.

The trader must determine in advance the best time to position and do not hesitate to go on the offensive when it occurs. Nevertheless, when markets are not predictable, the trader will have to avoid positioning himself and wait for the situation to clear up. He must have a clear view of the forces involved; as there is no point in exposing himself if so few favorable signals are present. Some traders explain that they simply want to test the markets by positioning themselves, but in truth, it is the market that tests them. Adapt to the situation.

trading by group

| BUY | % |
|---|---|
| 2,259.21 | 8.44% |
| 6,513.46 | 24.33% |
| 14,447.83 | 53.98% |
| 3,545.70 | 13.25% |

## Key Indices

| | PREVIOUS | CHANGE | |
|---|---|---|---|
| 91 | 977.22 | +8.69 | Energy & Utility |
| 58 | 1,488.55 | +15.03 | Fashion |
| 35 | 682.18 | +7.17 | Finance |
| 3 | 1,176.81 | +17.02 | Food & Beverage |
| 3 | 1,129.98 | +5.45 | Health Care |
| | 1,413.47 | +7.31 | Home & Office |
| 1,15 | 1,186.17 | +5.82 | Ind Material & M |
| 1,294 | 1,179.07 | +14.78 | Info & Comm Tec |
| 264.0 | 298.90 | -4.77 | Insurance |
| 281.64 | 61.09 | +2.96 | Media & P |
| 114.70 | 48 | +2.16 | Mines |
| 122.53 | | +0.29 | Packaging |

ons
Investors
vestors
tary trading

Small Cap
Mid/Small Cap
All-Share
Fledgling
Food
Product

Profession Services
Property Dev
Property Fund
Tour & Leisure
Transport & L

# Chapter 6

# Risk Considerations

In this chapter, we are going to take a quick look at some of the candlestick patterns that are important to you as a beginner. Understand that no individual pattern alone can give you all the clues you are looking for, so as I earlier mentioned, be sure to combine whatever information you deduce from a pattern with other information from other tools as well. The aim is to get a balanced perspective before jumping into conclusion. As a side note, it is not important that you cram the names of these patterns. What is most important is to know the appearances or the shapes of these patterns and what they mean.

## Bullish Patterns

This bullish pattern occurs on a stock chart when a hollow or white large candle engulfs a previous smaller filled or black candle; hence the name engulfing. The bullish engulfing pattern often occurs in a downtrend and when it does, there is a high chance of a reversal from the downtrend (bearish trend) to an uptrend (bullish trend). This pattern shows up to signify that active traders as well as investors have had a change of mind about the value of a stock and are beginning to be aggressive about it. This is what usually leads to a reversal in the stock's trend.

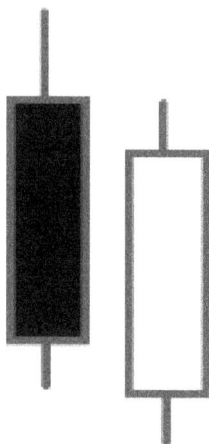

## Doji

This bullish pattern often shows hesitancy or indecisiveness in the minds of the traders. Usually, the stock price remains the same for the entire time frame after it opens. It closes almost at the same opening price. When this happens, there is likely to be a reversal of the trend in the opposite direction because traders are more than likely to doubt the price's dominant trend. In a dominant downward direction, the question in the traders' minds would be something along the lines of "why is the price not going down?" and this could possibly result in buying rushing to buy and causing prices to rise. There is no one single candlestick that has the entire messages you need to make your trading decision, but the Doji is a very significant candlestick you need to watch out for.

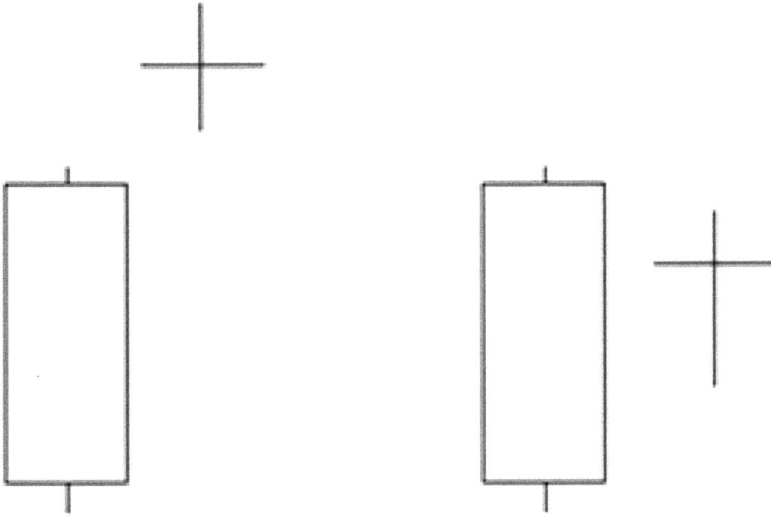

## Hammer

This occurs when traders begin to short-sell a stock after it opens. However, before closing, buyers force a reversal and the price closes at the top of the range. Sometimes hammer patterns show up when there have been considerable orders placed for a stop loss.

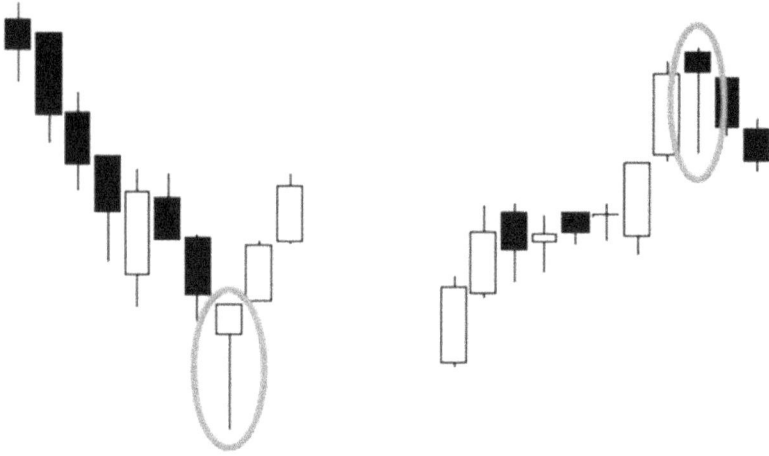

# Piercing

This pattern can also signify an imminent reversal. From a previous trading period, there usually is a wide range black candle which closes at the bottom of a range or near the bottom, signifying that sellers have the upper hand. But in the next trading period, a wide range white candle closes at a position that is somewhere halfway into the previous candle. Short sellers in the previous trading period are at a loss when this occurs.

## Piercing Line - Reversal

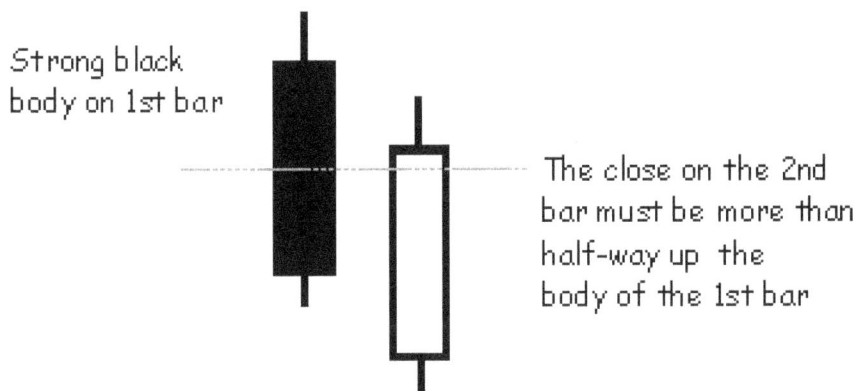

Strong black
body on 1st bar

The close on the 2nd
bar must be more than
half-way up the
body of the 1st bar

Reversal signal after a down-trend

# Harami

Harami means pregnant in Japan; hence, the Harami pattern usually shows up as two candles with the smaller one nestled inside the larger one. It can easily be mistaken for the engulfing pattern, but there are not the same. The positions of the candles are opposite that of the engulfing pattern. Usually, this pattern signifies a stop in preceding momentum. From a previous trading period, there usually is a wide range black candle which closes at the bottom of a range or near the bottom, signifying that sellers have the upper hand. However, in the next trading period, a narrow range white candle closes the period.

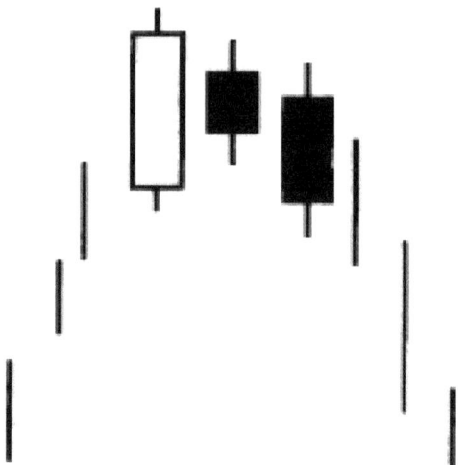

## Bearish Patterns

This bearish pattern occurs on a stock chart when a filled or black candle engulfs a previous smaller hollow or white candle. The bearish engulfing pattern often occurs in an uptrend to signify a likely reversal to a bearish trend or downtrend.

## Doji Star

The Doji Star is a bearish pattern that is formed by the appearance of a white wide range candle on the first day and followed by a Doji on the second day that gaps above the first day. The wigs of the Doji are not very long. This also signifies a possible reversal from an upward to a downward trend.

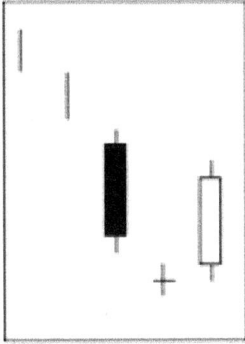

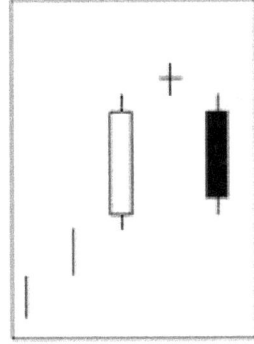

## Shooting Star

This bearish candle pattern looks like an inverted hammer pattern. It occurs when a stock's price goes above the opening price during the trading period, but at the closing, it came lower than the opening price. This bearish candle pattern is a good sign that an uptrend is losing steam; therefore it is a good idea to consider entering short trades when you see this pattern.

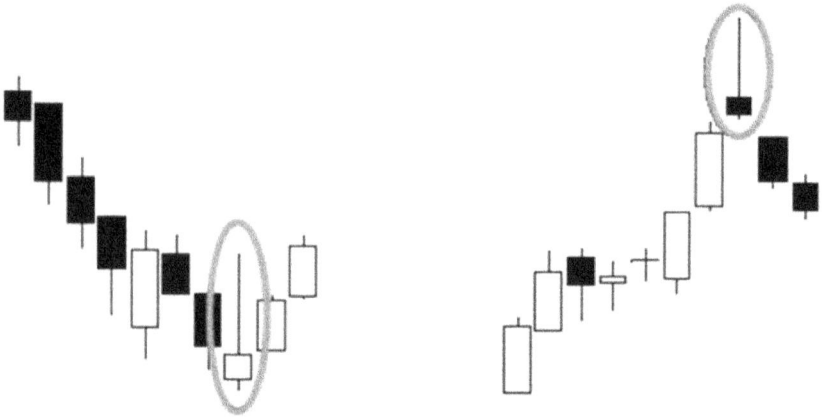

# Dark Cloud Cover

This bearish reversal pattern occurs when a filled (black) candle's opening price is above the closing price of a hollowed candle and is, at the same time, below the hollowed candle's midpoint.

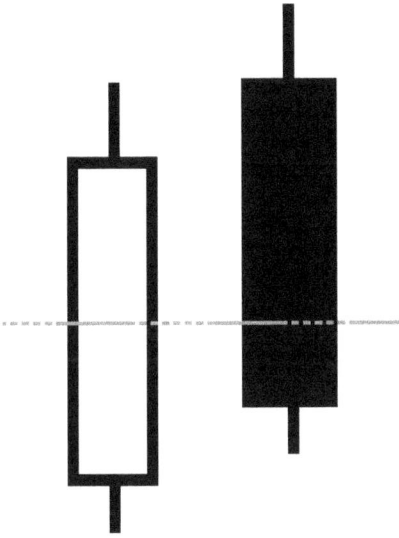

# Bearish Harami

This two-bar bearish candle pattern indicates a possible reversal to a downward trend. Obviously, an uptrend goes before a bearish Harami pattern occurs. Bearish Harami shows a hollow candle that is followed by a small filled candle. The opening price, as well as the closing price of the small filled (black) candle, has to be contained within the range of the hollow (white) candle.

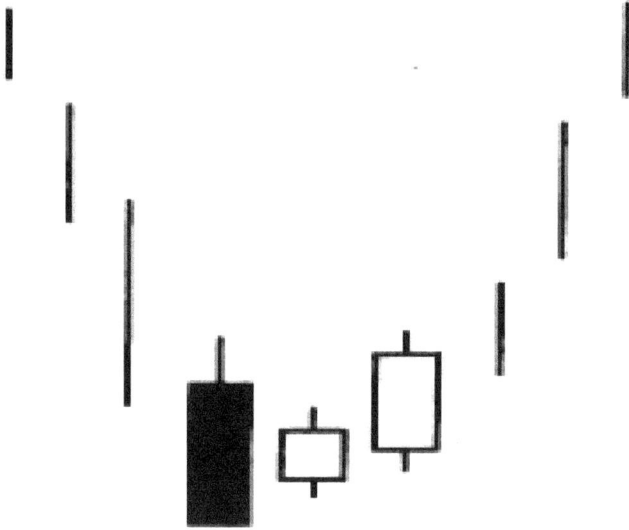

In summary:

- A wide range bullish candle signifies that buyers were actively buying and were therefore in charge of the trade during a larger part of the specified time frame.
- A wide range bearish candle means that sellers were vigorously selling and were more in charge of the trade for the most part of the trading duration.
- Narrow range candles show that neither buyers nor sellers were too passionate about the stock, therefore, creating a lesser impact on the opening price.
- A rather long tail at the bottom of a candle means that sellers were aggressive at the beginning of the time frame, however, before the close, buyers took the lead.

- A long tail at the top of a candle shows that buyers were tenaciously holding to their positions for a good part of the trading period. Nevertheless, sellers took over before the stock closed.
- When the body of a candle falls in between long upper and lower tails, it simply means that both buyers and sellers had an almost equal impact on the price of the stock. So trading appears balanced.

By now you should be able to look at a stock chart and, using what you have learned so far, understand exactly what the candlesticks are telling you.

## Using Two or More Candlesticks

Basing your options trading decision solely on the message of only one candlestick may not be a wise way to use candlesticks. Even if you do not fuse candlestick messages or signs with other tools, you should at least combine two or more candlesticks before taking any action.

Now, let us piece all of the patterns and all of the information about charts, trends, stages, waves, etc., together into charts and learn how to read them effectively. You will not be able to succeed as a swing trader without knowing how to read charts. The vital information you need to know before letting your money go into any trade is all in the chart. The chart tells you if the risk is worth it.

In order to get yourself familiarized with reading stock charts, you need to do this. Look for stock charts online and print them out. Now look at each stock chart and try to determine the following:

What trend is the stock on the chart? Is it going up (uptrend) or is it going down (downtrend)? Is the stock price falling or is it rising? What is the current stage of the stock? Is it in the first, second, third, or fourth stage? Can you determine the support and resistance points? Are there any signs of a breach? Is the trend of the stock a strong one? When was the last breakout? Has there been any pullback or rally? Is this the beginning, middle, or the end of the trend?

Practice with a good number of stock charts and you will definitely get better. With time, you wouldn't have to force yourself to remember these questions – they will occur to you as soon as you look at any chart and the answers will come to you as fast as you can think of the questions.

Let me break down what you should be looking for as you practice reading stock charts. Remember, in this beginners guide, we are using only the candlestick stock chart.

# Look for the Stock Trend or Chart Pattern

Firstly, train yourself to quickly identify the general stock direction (uptrend or downtrend) on the stock chart. I would suggest that you should adjust your daily chart to show the chart patterns dating back to about 7 to 8 months. The chart pattern for that time frame should show you clearly the trend, stages, and waves of the stock. When you have successfully identified a trend, you are ready to look for the next important thing on the stock chart.

# Look for the Price Pattern

Secondly, try to identify the price pattern of the stock. What you are looking for on a stock chart that you have identified as having an uptrend is a pullback. If you have identified the chart pattern as a downtrend, then what you are looking for is a rally. So, you've identified a chart pattern (stock trend) and you have found a pullback or rally depending on the direction of the trend. Now you will need to find one more piece to solve the puzzle.

# Look for the Candlestick Pattern

Lastly, look at what the candlesticks are saying. In an uptrend, if the pullback you observed in the price pattern is really a pullback, when the trend comes back around (returns to the dominant trend) the candlestick that should follow in an ideal situation would be a bullish candlestick such as the piercing, hammer, or an engulfing candlestick pattern. In a downtrend, if the rally you observed in the price pattern is really a rally, when the price movement returns to the dominant trend, the dark cloud cover, engulfing, or a shooting star are the likely bearish candlestick pattern that will follow the rally.

When you can effectively combine these three parts of a stock chart, you would have successfully learned one major aspect of reading stock charts.

## Technical Indicator: What It Is

The OHLC (open, high, low, and close) price of a stock over a period of time forms the price data of that stock or security. Now when the price data of a particular security is passed through a set of mathematical functions or formulas, a sequence of data points are created. This is what is known as a technical indicator. So to give it a proper definition: a technical indicator is a series or sequence of data points that are generated through the application of mathematical formulas to the price data of a particular security. Several other indices such as the volume of stock may also be included in the formula to generate the data points.

I am going to save you the headache of how the formula is applied to the price data and all the computations involved in coming up with a technical indicator. All you need to know as a beginner is that technical indicators are displayed graphically on top or below the chart of a security or stock. And it is there to aid you in your market analysis – to compare the stock's chart with the information on the technical indicator. The more in agreement they are, the better decision you can make.

Before you go hunting for the perfect technical indicator that will show you all the good trades, be aware that these indicators are not 100 percent accurate all of the time. They can signal a false buy or sell alert. So be warned.

# Functions and What You Get From Technical Indicators

Perhaps I should refresh your memory about moving averages. What did we say moving averages are used for? (Feel free to look back at chapter 4 to reacquaint yourself with moving averages.) We said the lines of a moving average indicate a stock's average price over a given period. So, they are basically indicators that show you the average price of a stock. Well, that's one thing you get from technical indicators.

While the stock chart shows you price action, technical indicators show you other information about the same stock from a different vantage point.

Anyone functions of technical indicators are summarized below:

- **For Confirmation:** Throughout this guide, I have advised that you should not base your trading decisions solely on one tool. A technical indicator can serve as a tool that you use in confirming whatever you deduce from price actions on a chart. For example, when you observe that a stock has broken a support level, you could look at the OBV to confirm if there is a low reading to indicate that there is an actual weakness. OBV means On Balance Volume; it is a technical indicator.

- **For Calling Attention:** Technical indicators can draw the trader's attention to study price actions more carefully. It can prompt you to a variety of alerts that can really save you from some serious financial damage. For example, you may be prompted to look out for a break in support level when momentum is declining.

- **For Predicting Price Direction:** A technical indicator can also serve as a tool for predicting what side future prices will lean towards – up or down.

## Proper Use of Technical Indicators

- **No One Size Fits All:** Different stocks may cause the same indicator to behave differently. In using technical

134

indicators, it is important to know that different indicators tend to work well for different stocks. With continuous practice and application, you will come to discover which indicator will serve you best for your chosen stocks.

- **To Indicate:** There is no single tool that has all the trading answers! Have I said that enough times yet? That is because it is of vital importance to keep that in mind. In that sense, it is important to note that one proper way to use a technical indicator is to see them as tools that only point to the likelihood of an outcome. They must be used in combination with price action. A technical indicator does not directly represent price action; what it does is to present you with information about its own generated or computed results from price data. There are times when a technical indicator will signal you to buy or sell, yet they could be very wrong. If you do not verify each signal with what the stock chart is telling you, it may lead to fatal trading mistakes. The bottom line is this: technical indicators aid you but they do not do the trading for you. Ultimately, you are the one who decides what and when to trade based on signals from indicators and other analysis.

- **Use Time Tested Indicators:** The proliferation of technical indicators seems to be on a constant rise. Some newer computer programs even provide users (traders) the choice of developing custom made indicators! But with all of the numerous new indicators available at our beck and call, it seems they do not offer anything too unique or new from others in existence before them. As a matter of fact, I would advise that as a beginner, you stick to time tested indicators to avoid being sent on a wild goose chase.

- **A Few Is Good Enough:** As mentioned above, there are several technical indicators available today. But you really do not need all of them. Heck! You do not even need more than three good technical indicators to succeed in a proper analysis. What matters is that you are well acquainted with the few you use. The fewer the number of indicators, the better you will learn and know how to use them.

- **A Few Complementary Indicators:** What would be the point of having three indicators that all function almost exactly the same way? That's a huge waste of time and resources. When you are picking out your few indicators, make sure that you select indicators that complement each other. That is to say, select indicators that perform functions that add to the functions of the other(s). If you decide to use only two indicators, for example, it doesn't make much sense to choose the Accumulation/Distribution Line and Chaikin Money Flow (CMF) as your only two technical indicators. Both of them perform the same function which is to show if money is coming in or going out of stock by combining volume and price.

# Learning the Options Trading Strategy

## Develop Your Trading Strategy

There is no perfect trading strategy; so stop searching for one. Moreover, you do not need a perfect trading strategy to make money from trading stocks. Ultimately, your trading strategy will be unique to you. However, as a beginner, you may need to lean a bit on an existing strategy in order to get the hang of it. With time, you can tweak things around to fit your particular trading style or build yours completely from scratch.

Here is a general idea you can use to build your own trading strategy.

# Preparation

You could start preparing for your trade at the beginning of a new week. Find out what types of trade (short or long) you will want to focus on. You could use a technical indicator such as the moving averages to determine this. After that, take a look at a few financial columns or news, reports, etc. This will give you the general outlook of how stocks are performing and what the market is up to. Look at charts of various industries to see stock strengths and weaknesses, plus promising stocks. Be sure to write down 9whatever catches your attention in your trading notepad (you don't have one yet?), because in the heat of trading, most things you note mentally won't come to your mind.

## Finding Stocks

Begin to search for potential trades by looking for stocks that:

- Have a strong trend
- Have shown first pullbacks or rallies
- Are at a resistance or support level
- Are in the second or fourth stages
- Are repeatedly touching a support or resistance area

If you do not find a trade that you are comfortable with as a beginner, please do not trade. Remember, trading involves going long, short, or staying in cash. So, learn to stay in cash if there is nothing appealing for you to trade.

## Double-Check

After you have found a trade, verify that the company whose stock you are about to trade is not going to release its earnings reports anytime soon. Trading a company's stock just before their earnings report is released can lead to a massive loss for you. So be sure to double-check. Here's one way you could find out.

Simply go to Yahoo Finance and type in the company's symbol. The date of the next earnings report will be shown.

## During Trades

All things checked and verified, start your trade. Do not give your attention to stock market news or other traders opinion during your own trades. Your attention needs to be only in one place: the stock chart. Ensure that you use trailing stops to closely follow your profits and that would be all you require during trades.

## Your Entry Strategy

Your money is at risk as soon as you enter a position to buy or sell a stock. So, you must be careful that you time your entry very well.

Your entry point should be at a swing point: a low swing point for buying, and a high swing point for selling.

A swing point is made up of three candles.

**Low Swing Point** (for entering a long position – buying)

- Candle one goes low
- Candle two goes lower than candle one (lower low)

- Candle three goes higher than candle two (higher low)

Candle three indicates that sellers are no more aggressive. This is a precursor for a trend reversal. This is your cue to enter a long position.

**High Swing Point** (for entering a short position – selling)

- Candle one goes high
- Candle two goes higher than candle one (higher high)
- Candle three goes lower than candle two (lower high)

Candle three indicates that buyers are no more aggressive. This is a precursor for a trend reversal. This is your cue to enter a short position.

# Successive Up Days or Down Days

Another way to enter a trade is to look for successive up days or down days. These are a lot easier to spot, but be sure that you are not entering the trade when the trend is about to end or reverse. Take a look at the chart below for a clearer understanding.

# Your Exit Strategy

You have read all the charts, and picked your stocks to trade and you have determined which market to trade on – in fact, you know exactly when to time your entry. But when do you exit a trade? When do you lock in profits? You see, as important as timing your entry is, if you neglect when to exit, you may not take any profits home after all.

You must plan well ahead of your entry how you intend to exit a trade. And remember that a plan is not a plan until it is written down. Following a plan in your head is the same as trading based on your emotions. It usually fails. Basically, there are three reasons why you should exit a trade, namely: when making profits, when losing money, and when you are not making or losing money.

Let us take a brief look at each of these reasons for exiting a trade.

# Taking Your Profits

Before you enter a trade, it is important to set a mechanism that tells you it is time to take your profits and exit the trade. Do not rely on some abstract feelings. Remember to be emotionally detached from your trade outcomes. That way, you will pay more attention to your previously set mechanism when it alerts you of an exit point. If you are greedy and wait too long, you may lose a substantial part of your profits. And if you are too fearful and quit too soon, you may equally lose a significant part of profits that should be yours. This boils down to emotional intelligence. The good news is that it can be developed. So if you intend to become a successful swing trader and you have determined that you do not have enough discipline to follow through with your plan, do not worry. You can learn how to do that as you take baby steps in options trading.

When you buy or sell a stock, ensure that you have a stop-loss point in mind. You can use that point to set a stop-loss order, or you can click buy or sell when prices get to that point.

## Ending Your Losses

Make up your mind long before you enter any trade that you are going to cut your losses early enough before it digs a hole in your account that will require a lot of money to mend. Again, you have to set up a prior mechanism for identifying when to cut your losses. I strongly suggest that you use the trailing stops to cut losses. Set your losses to somewhere around 3% (or less) of your capital. Make your losses are as small as possible so you don't get all emotional about the loss.

Be on the lookout for repeated price attempts to breach support or resistance. That is an indication of a possible breakout.

Sticking to a losing position in the hope of it rebounding is abandoning your plans and listening to your emotions. In options trading, hope doesn't give you profits. Most often than not, hope has an ironic way of crippling your account.

## Freeing Up Your Capital

Whether you choose to quickly exit a trade that is neither making you money nor making you lose money, or you choose to watch it for a few days, both choices are okay. The important thing is that before you enter the trade, you should make up your mind about how long you are willing to watch a trade that is generally lukewarm. Remember that you are in a type of trade that is considered short-term. You don't have the whole month to wait for one position. If it is tying down your money, free up your capital and reinvest it in another stock or position.

## Trading Pullbacks and Rallies

As earlier discussed, pullbacks and rallies are great opportunities to buy and sell stocks (in case you missed it, you can check it out in chapter 3).

Usually, when stock prices begin to move in an upward direction (an uptrend), they tend to briefly pullback. This presents you a good opportunity to buy at low risk and increases your chances of selling at a higher price later. On the reverse side, when stock prices begin to move in a downward direction (downtrend), they tend to briefly rally and offer you an excellent opportunity for shorting.

Here is something for you to consider as a beginner in options trading. If all you do is simply stay in cash (that is, holding on to your money without trading) until you find excellent pullbacks and rallies, you will be making a wise beginner decision.

Think about it. It stands to reason that the best time to buy stocks at a great price is right after a recent occurrence of selling. It equally shows better judgment to short sell right after the occurrence of buying.

The best time to trade pullbacks and rallies is the first time they appear on a chart after a significant trend. So the first time you notice a pullback after a trend line is breached or broken, seize the opportunity. Be on the lookout for a pullback that happens immediately following a wide range candle. Buy or sell at that point. When you see a breakout, be ready to trade the first pullback after it. When a new high is set, wait for the first pullback. When it comes up, go in for the kill.

Let us look at the chart below to get a clearer picture of the above. The first pullback after a significant downtrend offered those who were watchful an excellent opportunity to buy early.

# You Cannot Win All Trades

No, you can't. It doesn't matter what tools or magic formula you use. Remember that the stock market contains so many moving parts that are far beyond the control of any one individual or a body. Any of these moving parts could have a significant adverse effect on even the best technical indicators or analysis tools.

But you can win a lot of trades enough to make you good profits. The profits you make come from the ignorance or mistakes of other traders. In the stock market, you are either making mistakes or you are making profits. Unfortunately for most traders, they are making mistakes. Whether you will choose to make profits depends largely on if you will take your learning seriously to avoid the mistakes most novices make.

Some of these mistakes are depending 100% on technical analysis, being too afraid to lose, looking for a fail-proof system or trading magic formula, being emotional, etc. The truth is, not everyone is cut out to be a trader or a swing trader. However, a lot of people will give it a shot and eventually fail. It is from these failed attempts that you will make profits if you learn and apply what these other traders won't.

You will not win all your trades, but you will win a lot of your trades provided you do not buy and sell as the novices do. When do you time your buys? At the beginning of a pullback or when the crowd has said it is okay to buy? At what times do you sell? When you notice a rally or when major selling is almost over? You see, buying or selling too late is the hallmark of novices, which a lot of traders are, no matter how long they have spent trading. The number of years a trader spends trading the stock market does not necessarily make them experts. It is what you learn and applies that distinguishes you from the novices.

Stand apart by trading in the opposite direction of the crowd. Don't worry, expert and veteran traders don't usually trade in the direction of the crowd, so you are not making a mistake when you do so. But when the crowd is selling – the prices are a lot cheaper then. And of course, you know very well to sell when the crowd is buying, the price is a lot higher then because everyone wants to get the hot-selling stocks which you happen to have.

## Options Trading Is a Continuous Learning Process

There are challenges you will encounter as you trade. You do not improve if you quit or if you stop only at what you have learned so far. Becoming a swing trader means you are going to keep learning on a continuous basis in order to bring on your A-game.

It is important to recognize the dynamism of the market. The market doesn't stay still for too long. For you to be anything close to success in the art of options trading, you must be ready to continue adapting to changes in rules, regulations, and laws. Additionally, new and exciting vehicles of investments keep springing up. Stay up to speed with new information about the market.

There is money to be made from options trading, but you must be ready to do your part by continuously learning new ways to make money. You should see options trading as an art of improving your trading skills rather than a way of making money. The money part is a natural result of making good trades. You cannot flop on your trades out of ignorance and expect to make money. It is not out of line to assume that the amount of profit you generate from options trading is directly proportional to your options trading skill level. The more you improve, the more profits flood your account. And you certainly cannot improve without keeping yourself abreast of up-to-date information about stocks, prices, markets, etc.

As part of your learning, you will encounter situations that will teach you better than any book the art of accepting losses. You may follow every single detail in your well mapped out strategy or plan, yet you will still lose a trade. It is not time to argue with the losses or stubbornly hold on to the position. Accept it. You have lost. It happens. Now dust yourself up and try again this time, more intelligently.

Remember that you are a swing trader who is supposed to study the psychology of traders. You are supposed to leverage the emotional shortcomings of other traders and make profits. You cannot successfully do that if you have not mastered your own emotions. Continuing to trade with the aim of breaking even when you are losing is a gateway to financial disaster. Avoid it by all means.

I will not fail to add that you must shield yourself from the herd mentality. You must distinguish yourself from the trading crowd. Do not follow the crowd unless you have determined by yourself that they are towing the right direction (which is not a very common occurrence both in options trading and any other aspect of life). And the reason why herd mentality is not good for you is that the herds do not think for themselves. They depend on one person's or one organization's opinion. These opinions were thought of by human traders (even if they used computerized tools to draw their conclusions). You are capable of reaching your own opinions too. Herd mentality is generated from the internet, message board, and even so-called guru analysts.

Nevertheless, do not discard time-tested facts about the market in the guise of shielding yourself from the herd mentality. That is why I would recommend that you find reliable sources of information so that you can digest them and draw your own conclusions.

# Finally, Learn Some Basic Money Management

A lot of people win the lottery by chance (how else would you win a lottery if not by chance!), but they still become broke after a few weeks, months or a couple of years? Why is that so? They do not have basic money management skills. It doesn't matter how much money you make from the stock market (or from winning the lottery!), if you do not have money management skills, you are simply exposing yourself to trade like a gambler or someone buying a lottery ticket – you will begin trading in the hope that you will win (like a game of chance) because you are under pressure to make money you have previously lost due to bad money management policies.

## Contract

A contract allows portfolio managers and companies to hedge against random events.

For example, a French company that exports to the United States and bills in dollars may have an interest in blocking the selling price as of now. It will, therefore, ask its treasurer to sell future contracts for an amount equivalent to the exported goods, so as to block its selling price (which has many advantages, because the company knows now its costs, but also future cash inflows).

Suppose the price in it is the following: 1 $ = 1 €. The company planned to export $ 10 million worth of goods over the year. If the price of the euro falls to the level of $ 0.90, in the event that the company did not cover these sales, it would have lost one million euros (0.10 x 10 million).

The main advantage of futures is to allow hedging. For this, these markets must be liquid and speculators will represent the counterpart and therefore bear the risk. The liquidity of the futures markets is mainly due to the presence of many speculators in the electronic markets. Henceforth, the absence of intermediaries on the floors makes these instruments perfect vehicles for intraday speculation. In addition, brokerage fees, due to recent technological advances, have collapsed allowing an individual to become profitable from the first tick.

The most famous contracts with day traders are the E-mini Nasdaq 100 and the E-mini S & P 500, which are traded on the Chicago Mercantile Exchange. Orders are placed electronically and executed almost automatically. More recently, we have seen the appearance of the mini-Dow. In Europe, the most traded contracts on stock market indices are Dax, Footsie, and CAC21.

The value of a CAC point is 10 euros and the minimum deposit is 2,250 euros (negotiable for intraday). The value of a Nasdaq E-mini point is $20, and the minimum deposit is $ 3,250 ($ 2,500 for intraday or even $ 500 / $ 300 with some brokers). The value of a E-mini S & P 500 is $50, and the minimum deposit is $ 3,500 ($ 500 for intraday).

These future contracts have many advantages:
- The trader follows only a few indices instead of following dozens of actions;
- These markets are extremely liquid, and it is, therefore, possible to get in and out very quickly of its positions. Moreover, thanks to the passage of electronic orders, orders are executed almost instantaneously.
- Leverage is important. It is usually 20 but can easily reach 100 with some brokers.

## The Hybrid Method

Some traders consider that the optimal system combines both approaches. Jesse Livermore's method is interesting in that it capitalizes on the concept "the trend is your ally". She considers that it is possible to miss several small movements, but we must never miss a strong trend because the bulk of the profits are made in this type of market. Nevertheless, it does not allow the trader to quickly take profits while this attitude should be favored when the market is without a trend.

We have developed a method taking into account the contributions of the two methods (the classical method and that of Livermore). If the trader has a strong conviction about a title, he can open the entire position at the very beginning and take his profits after an average boost (example: 10%) on half of the position and ride his stop. If the stock consolidates and offers a new interesting entry point then we can ride the stop under the previous support and increase our position.

This system takes the best of the other two. We secure profits when the stock moves in the expected direction and we continue to capitalize on the current trend with the profits made at the first momentum. The first movement will be a net winner and the second should be neutral if the position is stopped.

To summarize, rigorous risk management is necessary to survive in the markets, but it assumes that the trader strictly complies with the following points:

- He must only retain opportunities offering a Risk / Reward of at least 3 positions (therefore a potential gain three times greater than the tolerated loss);

- Diversification of investments for a swing trader. Any market operator can set romper on the evolution of the markets. Diversification reduces the risk of error by betting more uncorrelated contracts, rather than bet on one with the risk of suffering a consequential loss in the event of adverse movement;

- The specialization for the day trader and the scalper. The trader must avoid opening more than three positions at a time and focus on a few titles in order to be totally focused on the process. Diversification is not necessary because the positions are closed before the end of the day. The most important for the trader remains the perfect knowledge of the main technical levels (supports, resistances, Fibonacci ratio ...) in order to operate in the most efficient way;

- Ideally, the tolerable loss on a position should never exceed 1 to 2% of the capital, but this percentage will also depend on the size of the capital and the strategy adopted.

# The Strategic Dimension of Trading

The strategy consists of developing an action plan, defined according to the strengths and weaknesses, taking into account the threats and opportunities observed by the protagonist. The strategy was first a war science, but soon found many other areas of application. The art of trading has many similarities with the art of war.

The armies that win are those whose general master the art of strategy. Likewise, the most successful investors are true strategists. "The market is an arena where other traders are opponents." – Martin Schwartz

Trading represents a fight between buyers (who want the market to rise) and sellers (whose main objective is to lower prices), whose ultimate objective is to grab the resources of the other party. There are many similarities between war and trading. According to Sun Tzu, the first objective of the war is not to humiliate and shed blood within the ranks of his opponent, but above all to ensure his survival and win by avoiding unnecessary deaths. Similarly, in terms of trading, the strategy aims essentially to achieve a pure monetary performance, while taking a little risk and ensuring that the results are not very volatile.

Sun Tzu has enunciated five principles of victory that apply in our opinion perfectly to the art of trading: knowing when it is appropriate to fight, and when it is appropriate to withdraw (defend); know how to use the little and the most according to the circumstances (save your resources and use them intelligently); to skillfully match his ranks (discipline); he who, prudent, prepares to face an enemy who is not yet; he himself will be victorious. To take advantage of its rusticity and not to foresee is the greatest crime; to be ready without any contingency is the greatest of virtues (to be perfectly prepared); to be safe from the interference of the sovereign in all that one can attempt for his service and the glory of his arms (to have an independence of mind)

To succeed in the markets, the trader must know himself perfectly and therefore understand the role played by emotions before, during and after the taking of a position: it is about his survival. Similarly, it will allow him to understand the behavior of other traders and capitalize on it.

Indeed, the trader operates in a very often virtual way and sometimes alone. It has real-time information flows and must position itself according to specific criteria. The precepts developed by authors like Sun Tzu provide extremely useful elements to help the trader to be totally focused on his task. What could be better than to think of yourself as the general of an army that must be led to victory? Nevertheless, this comparison is not only done in a motivational perspective, but it also provides valuable insights on the attitude to adopt in trading. The words developed in the art of war perfectly apply to the world of business and trading.

On a psychological level, the fact that a trader represents himself as a strategist can help him to increase his discipline. A positive personal image plays an important role in the success of the trader and this is all the more true as trading is a virtual world where competitors are not always known.

To illustrate this, let's take the example of a market that is falling sharply. The common traders will panic and seek to rush out of a position or sell. A good trader will first analyze the situation and coldly evaluate the interest of positioning. If the conditions look good then he will not hesitate to do so. Similarly, like the general who leads an army, the trader should not be stubborn and do not hesitate to retreat if it is the most favorable outcome, even if he returns to the battlefield by the following.

## The Main Categories of Investors

Behavioral finance (NTA) has highlighted three categories of investors:

The rational investor is the one who controls the fundamentals, but who also takes into account the reaction of other investors to market information. He acts as a strategist.

The fundamentalist investor relies essentially on fundamentals to position himself, in this sense; he is passive on the markets and is not a strategist.

Ignorant investors, or noise traders, have no strategy and only follow mass movements. Their expectations are formed in an unreasonable way. They will rely on weak signals (they ignore the probabilities and operate on instinct) to intervene and use popular models such as technical analysis to act.

For behavioral finance, an investor should be concerned about the views of other traders even when it differs from the fundamental value. Indeed, this opinion can considerably influence prices when it receives a sufficiently large membership. Thus, prices can shift in a sustainable and significant way compared to fundamentals solely due to sheep phenomena and other beliefs of ignorant investors. According to the behaviorists, the rational investor must take advantage of the behavior of ignorant investors.

# Chapter 7

# Risk & Money Management

## The Rhythmic and Cyclical Markets

Ralph Nelson Elliott has developed an approach to interpret wave market movements. His work focuses on hourly Dow Jones quotations and is released from 1938, arousing interest due to the emergence of fractals and chaotic movements.

This analysis considers an alternation between unpredictable periods and deterministic periods. Markets would not be governed by a random walk as Burton Malkiel mentioned. Mandelbrot develops this aspect in his book Fractals, chance, and finance. He considers that the evolution of prices is discontinuous, that prices can shift suddenly, and not in a gradual and continuous way, like good weather and bad weather in short: "If the markets were perfect, they would react instantly to all the news," he exclaimed. Now, they sometimes take time to integrate information and sometimes do so with exaggeration.

Elliott's research leads him to the following conclusion: the continual changes in the stock market reflected a fundamental harmony of nature. Thus, he notes that variations in the Dow Jones Industrial Average (DJIA) construct visible figures that return in the same forms, although they may vary in duration and amplitude.

These observations will allow him to develop a theory, known as Elliott's Wave Theory. It combines the psychological dimension borrowed from Charles Dow and the harmony of nature identified by the mathematician Fibonacci. It consists of a set of empirical rules to interpret the evolution of the main stock indices. This tool is powerful because the rules and principles stated by Elliott are supposed to contain all the action of the market. The main advantage of the Elliott Wave Method is to set up scenarios, set targets and has points of invalidation, the universe of possibilities being known.

This approach is very interesting because it allows one to consider the cyclicality of the financial markets. Indeed, stock prices evolve in a cyclical way: a rise or a fall will never appear in time and will be punctuated by movements of consolidation or correction. Elliott was one of the first writers to highlight the concept of action/reaction which posits that each impulsive movement must be followed by a corrective movement, the impulsive movement being more important in amplitude than the corrective movement.

For example, in an uptrend, the amplitude of impulsive (bullish) waves is generally stronger than that of corrective waves (downs) and vice versa.

During a marked trend, it seems obvious that the market can blow after an impulsive movement. This phenomenon can easily be explained by profit-taking. New entrants (buyers in an uptrend and sellers in a downtrend) are waiting for the presence of a low point to position themselves, which will allow the resumption of the dominant trend. The great strength of Elliott's waves is to be a complete method that emphasizes the two most important elements in trading that are price and time.

## Elliott Wave Decomposition

In various articles that were published in the Financial World in 1939, Elliott indicated that the market's bottom rate was a cycle of eight waves, containing five waves of the rise and three waves of decline. The three waves of decline are a correction of the five previous waves of increase.

For Elliott, every impulsive movement is followed by a corrective movement. An impulsive movement is composed of five waves of a lower degree of which three are impulsive and two are corrective. The corrective movement is composed of three waves, two of which are corrective, and one is impulsive.

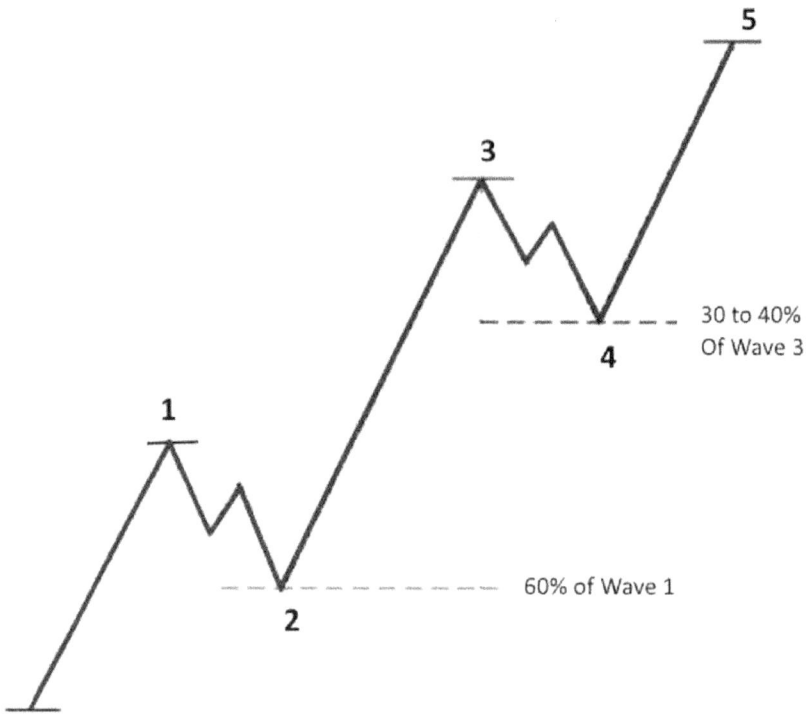

We will first describe the decomposition of the five waves contained in the impulsive movement:

The first wave represents the arrival of precursors on the markets. The latter anticipates the market turnaround and the imminence of an impulsive movement. They seek to return at the very beginning of the movement and correspond to the initiated investors mentioned by Charles Dow.

The second wave very often corresponds to a strong correction of the first impulsive movement. It represents the entry of contrarians who play the decline because they believe that the market remains in a bearish phase.

The third wave is usually that of followers and professional investors. The news is positive and the operators are rushing on the title, causing a strong upward acceleration. It's the most powerful impulsive wave, and it's never the shortest.

The fourth wave is profit-taking by operators who took advantage of the sharp rise in a wave. Nevertheless, the trend remains bullish and it is not questioned.

The fifth wave is the last impulsive wave of major impulsive movement. It corresponds to the entry of late followers, who have observed the rise without positioning themselves and who are eager to enjoy the movement like others. Generally, they are the first victims of the market downturn. This wave is also characterized by a depletion of the technical indicators which often draw a bearish divergence and point the breathlessness of the trend in progress and the imminence of a correction.

On many impulsive waves, it is not uncommon to note the presence of an "extension": it is a wave of impulse which is prolonged and which marks the power of the wave in question. This extension usually takes shape on a single impulsive wave, which allows analysts to take the measure of other waves. Thus, if the first and third waves are of the same length, the fifth will certainly be an extension. The rules set out by Elliott are supposed to contain all the action of the market.

According to Elliott, this decomposition is found whatever the period is chosen. Some analysts do not hesitate to make a comparison with the theory of chaos, developed especially by Mandelbrot. According to this theory, there would be an order in apparent disorder, and images taken at different scales (short term, long term) may have striking similarities. They forget, however, that the principal concerned, Mandelbrot, does not take Elliott's waves seriously. But let us leave aside these sterile quarrels and interest us in the most important: this method is popular, it is followed (the trader must, therefore, integrate it into his arsenal) and it is even sometimes effective!

## Four Basic Principles and Five Rules

There are several principles governing Elliott's waves, which we will summarize into basic principles:

Action is followed by a reaction: markets never go up in a single time; the impulse waves, movements in the direction of the primary tendency, break down into five waves of a lower degree, and the corrective waves, movements against the primary trend (bullish or bearish), are decomposed into three waves of a lower degree;

When a movement in eight waves (five up and three down) ends, a complete cycle comes to an end, and this cycle becomes two subdivisions in the immediately higher degree wave; whatever the time horizon, the way of counting is the same because the market is moving at the same pace. The rules stated must imperatively be applied during a count and will be controlled over time.

## Corrective Waves

There are several types of corrective waves (zigzags, flats, etc.). In a 5-step movement, corrective waves always correct the previous upward movement. The following properties are the most commonly observed: wave 2 corrects wave 1 and wave 4 corrects wave 3. Elliott, along with several top-flight analysts, noted that corrective waves regularly corrected the impulsive movements of a certain percentage.

FLAGS

"BULL" FLAG
IN AN UPTREND

"BEAR" FLAG
IN A DOWNTREND

PENNANTS...

...IN AN UPTREND
(BULLISH)

...IN A DOWNTREND
(BEARISH)

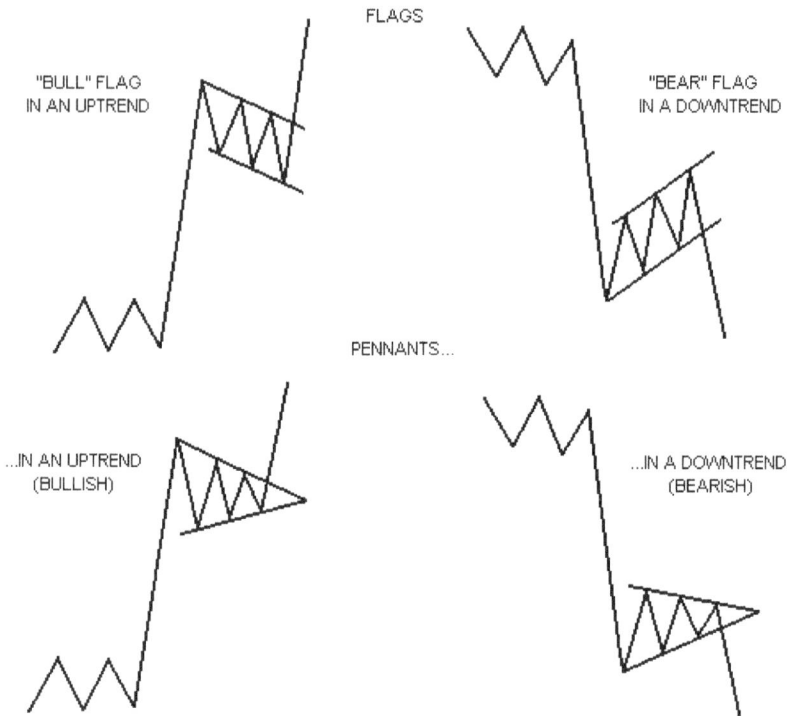

# Standard Wave Retracement Ratios 2

Wave 2 is often the strongest and corrects waves 1. It traces the previous move at a minimum of 38.2% to 50%, but the standard retracement is 61.8% and can go up to a maximum of 76.4%.

# Standard Wave Retracement Ratios 4

Wave 4 represents profit-taking. The correction is never strong and stands at least 23.6%, the standard is 38.2% and they never retrace more than 50%. If the correction is greater than 50% then it is probably necessary to question its count because it is probably a wave 1.

In summary, Wave 2 corrects strongly (61.8% is the standard ratio); while Wave 4 is profit-taking (the standard ratio is often 38.2%).

# Can We Distinguish A Corrective Wave From A True Reversal Of The Trend?

We have previously seen that an uptrend could be called into question when a lower precedent was depressed. A correction was then drawn, and the prices have depressed the two previous low points without that preventing the title from continuing its ascent. Indeed, this corrective movement corrects the entirety of the previous movement.

The corrective movement corresponds to a true reversal of the trend if and only if the corrective wave sinks the low point of the previous impulsive movement. If not, the current trend remains healthy and nothing comes to question it.

# The Rule of Alternation

This rule is a powerful principle of Elliott's waves. The principle is simple: if a wave 2 corrects strongly, then the correction in wave 4 will be weaker. Conversely, if wave 2 corrects weakly, expect an impulsive wave 3 but also a correction in wave 4 powerful.

The second property of alternation rules is based on the simplicity or complexity of the correction. At a wave 2 simple usually follows a complex wave 4. Conversely, if Wave 2 is complex then Wave 4 will be simple.

# Impulsive Waves

Impulsive waves are linked together by Fibonacci ratios. Thus, the objective of wave 3 is often obtained in the following way: we multiply the length of the wave 1 by 1.618 and we postpone the result obtained on the bottom of the wave 2. Often, wave 3 will go to hit this objective before correcting in wave 4. But during powerful movements in extension, the ratio will be higher than 1,618. The following ratios are usually taken: 2-2,618-3 and so on.

If wave 2 is weakly traced (less than 50%), expect a powerful wave 3 and project it with ratios above the standard of 1.618.

# Advantages

The main advantage of Elliott's method of waves is that it forces the analyst and the trader to imagine different counts, which is an excellent preparation to face the different eventualities.

A good "elliottist" is never closed, and he will always highlight in his analysis a favorite scenario (the one that has the best chance of unfolding) and an alternative (a scenario that would invalidate his ideal scenario).

## Disadvantages

The first disadvantage of Elliott waves is the learning time they require. Does the time devoted to training Elliott's waves necessarily find a justification?

I will answer that it may be interesting for a trader to know the basics of Elliott's waves and their fundamentals, but that the signals provided by this method do not seem sufficiently convincing to devote too much time.

The waves of Elliott fascinate many stakeholders, so much so that they become slaves. This method makes it possible to identify turning points with a confusing precision. Nevertheless, the trap of this method of analysis is to force the countdown in a situation where none seems apparent. The analyst then stubbornly searches for movements in five times where there are none.

This danger is well illustrated by the well-known Elliott Wave Advisor Prechter, who became famous in 1987 for predicting the stock market crash with this method. In the 1990s, his market diagnosis was extremely negative and he hammered in all the media that the US market was about to enter a prolonged bearish phase. This analyst was trapped by his method. He fell in love with it instead of considering it for what it really is: a simple analytical tool.

The moral of this story is two-fold: the markets are always right, and the trader who fights against this reality may pay very dearly.

## Graphical Analysis

Graphical analysis (also known as chart analysis) is a method that aims to identify the levels of media and resistances on a graph, as well as the current trend, through the tracing of trend lines and channels. This long-standing and well-known method owes its existence to operators and analysts who have studied the stock market charts and taken care to postpone in writing the recurring configurations, thus creating a directory of the most widespread configurations on the financial markets used by the vast majority of investors.

As with other methods of technical analysis, these figures can effectively capture the dominant sentiment in a market, even if their effectiveness is largely explained by the phenomenon of self-fulfilling prophecies. Indeed, these figures are known stakeholders, and their occurrence will often be the cause of a reaction that can be noted on the stock chart. Thus, resistance will not necessarily cause a downward reversal of the current trend but it can slow it down, even slightly. This reaction around key levels will need to be seriously analyzed by stakeholders.

Graphical analysis is an important tool in any trader's arsenal, but it is also risky and should be used with caution. The trader must avoid at all costs a too rigid reading. Indeed, a good trader's own strength is flexibility, and technical analysis should in no way be considered an exact science. From then, around support, the trader does not have to rush to buy. It must consider all the technical elements and the market context before making a decision. Similarly, when a support is broken, the trader must always ask if it is a break in front to be taken seriously or simply a false signal that he will have to ignore.

- What are the main graphic figures?
- How is a graphic figure validated?
- How to guard against false signals generated by these figures?

# Supports and Resistances

## Support (Media)

A medium can be defined as a level that supports the market and has been marketed many times in the past. Nevertheless, this definition is restrictive because round figures and Fibonacci retracements can also support the market without necessarily being affected before.

The strength of support can be explained by the following elements:

Around support, the buyers are more powerful than the sellers and manage to counter the progress of the bears; a support is an ideal level to position itself for the purchase for a trader whose market diagnosis is bullish, or for a profit-taking by an operator who is seller; bullish traders generally place their stops behind the main graphical media for an obvious reason: the breaking of the medium invalidates their bullish scenario and makes it possible to exit at a correct level; the importance of this graphic level is all the stronger as it is observed by most operators. The market often reacts around these levels, which makes some economists say that the reliability of technical analysis is primarily due to self-fulfilling beliefs.

Beware, in today's markets, many operators manipulate these levels in order to trigger stops. Media should, therefore, be used prudently by traders. Their reliability is fragile, and the trader will have to rely on other graphic and technical signals to support his scenario.

## Resistance

Resistance is a level against which the market has stumbled several times. Several elements explain the effectiveness of this level graph:

Around a resistance, sellers are more powerful than the buyers and manage to counter the bull's advances; this level attracts sellers short on the market because it is a good opportunity with a low risk: the stop is close and the bearish potential can be important; buyers, meanwhile, anticipate a consolidation, or even a correction of the title and take their profits or completely out of their positions;

As for the supports, the signals given by resistance can induce a trader in error. This level is observed by most operators; professional traders know this and voluntarily promote false signals (breaking resistance) in order to provoke the panic of the novices they know how to profit from.

Resistance will generally support the market when it is exceeded. Stakeholders remember this level and know that the bulls won the fight. They will, therefore, take advantage of this return on the support (old resistance) to initiate low-risk buying positions.

# Detailed Analysis of the Supports and the Resistances

This analysis is of great importance: the trader must get used to considering the different possible alternatives and must at all costs avoid the search for certainty. By having in mind the different possible reactions of the title around resistance or support, the trader will not be disappointed or surprised if his position results in a loss.

Around a significant resistance, the title can react in several ways and we have classified the possible reactions into four main categories:

1. The title breaks against resistance before drawing a major correction. This resistance indicates the presence of a high point and signifies a major reversal of the current trend;
2. The title draws a slight consolidation around the resistance before taking the path of the rise. This level could be used by traders positioned to buy to take their profits, but certainly not to sell. The current trend is not in

question and the trader must strive to play this movement in all its amplitude;

3. After a slight hesitation, the title ends up breaking the resistance but does not manage to stay very long above this new support. It is downward refractory and is on a downward path. This is a typical case of false signal that can prove fatal for a poorly prepared trader.

4. This situation is generally delicate and frustrating for a trader. It is not common, but when it is formed, it can cause real damage. The trader, in this situation, is often "wandered" by the market and loses control of his emotions. It must, therefore, take the distance and always favor a convergence of signals before positioning.

# The Effectiveness of Supports and Resistances

Supports and resistances attract stakeholders for obvious reasons: these levels generally correspond to round figures or levels on which the market has been asked several times. They can represent a significant barrier that hinders bearish movements and blocks progress.

Their importance is even greater in situations where the market is without a marked tendency. Some traders have even specialized in buying media and selling resistors in this type of market.

Supports and resistors are areas around which many operators are positioned or are already positioned. It is for this reason that emotions are easily exacerbated around these levels. Many traders are trapped by their psychological bias (bias momentum, anchor bias, etc.) and their emotions quickly take over, whether in winning or losing position.

A trader who sees a title down thinks that the movement will continue and rushes to sell it. Similarly, a person who has sold security around support [a common occurrence when a person rushes to sell security] will panic when the security goes up and participate in the bullish move by seeking to close his position as soon as possible.

The strength of the supports and the resistance rests on the observation according to which these levels are observed by most of the operators, and it is for this reason that the stock prices mark most of the time a stop around these levels. Nevertheless, the break will be more or less marked according to the current trend and the importance of support or resistance. In a strong trend market, the break will be short and the market will irremediably continue its trend without really catching a breath.

To summarize, the importance of supports and resistances will depend on the configuration of the market:

- **In a bull market,** resistances will be levels used exclusively to take profits and certainly not to sell a security. The media will be privileged to position themselves for the purchase;
- **In a bear market,** the trader will have to adopt the opposite attitude. The supports will be used exclusively to take profits or to cut a short position. They will never be used to initiate a long position. On the other hand, resistances will be relevant levels to open a new short position or increase an existing short position;
- **In a market without trend,** the operators are undecided, and the market will hit the main support/resistance. In this market configuration, the supports and the resistances will be of crucial importance and will have to be taken into account.

# The Importance of Round Figures as Supports / Resistances

Many authors and practitioners have highlighted the importance of round figures as supports/resistances: they attract the attention of stakeholders and cause an accumulation of new orders and profit-taking; they do not require special skills in technical analysis. Anyone involved, regardless of their original training (technical analysis, fundamental analysis, etc.), will naturally take as references round figures for obvious reasons of convenience.

For these different reasons, most operators are positioning themselves around these levels, or at least monitoring them, because they know that other stakeholders are doing the same and that a reaction around them is likely.

## The Courses Have a Memory

The courses have a memory and that is the reason why a resistance or support remains valid even if they have not been touched for a long time. During the corrective phases, it is not uncommon for a stock to land on a medium that has not been touched for four or five years and stabilizes around before resuming the upward path.

# Chapter 8

# Position Analysis

Swing trading is an approach based on the observation that stock prices never evolve linearly. An increase never takes shape in some time, and it is often punctuated by corrective phases. As per the experts, the basic trading philosophy can be summarized as follows:

- The best opportunities lie in detecting low-risk entry points in the direction of the prevailing trend. Thus, in an uptrend, the trader will have to wait for a correction or consolidation before positioning himself for the purchase.

- Conversely, in a downward trend, the trader will have to position himself only after a rebound around a significant resistance.

In the 1980s, a hedge fund manager went in the same direction by making famous the concept of contraction/expansion. It highlights the NR7 (or smaller range of the last seven days) and specifies that a consolidating market should accelerate just after the appearance of NR7.

Wilder and Appel are the two most cited authors for technical indicators. They introduced mathematics in technical analysis through the development of some technical indicators, very popular in trading rooms.

These indicators are based on different mathematical formulas inspired by physics. The main thesis of these authors is that the speed of an object thrown in the air is reduced as and when its progression, to become zero on the tops. They argue that market movements can be anticipated through these indicators, whose main function is to take the pulse of the market and answer the question: "The current trend - Is it intact or exhausting?"

These first steps have been relayed in the financial world and are the cause of the emergence of technical analysis and many technical indicators of development. People have always been fascinated by the world of trading however with the risks involved, it can get to be a daunting task. Understanding the stock market and paying attention to the different kinds of trading options can be very stressful. This book will help you understand the basics of swing trading and how you can benefit from it.

# Diversification and the Choice of Markets

Diversification is a common-sense concept, which consists of not putting all your eggs in one basket. In our opinion, this approach applies mainly to traders who have a swing trading perspective (medium and long term) but does not seem suitable for short-term traders such as day traders and scalpers. The latter generally focus on a few titles or contracts that they master perfectly and on which they play low amplitude movements.

# The Importance of Diversification

The risk of high bankruptcy in trading requires any operator to aim first and foremost the protection of its capital, and in this perspective to ensure that the risks are limited. At any moment, an unexpected event can make him lose a big part of his capital. (Crash, warning on results, extremely negative news).

The concept of diversification is based on the idea that any market operator can be mistaken about the evolution of the markets. Diversification is a way to reduce the risk of error by betting on several uncorrelated contracts rather than relying on a single contract. Some opportunities seem more promising than others and will encourage traders to significantly increase their exposure. Should we increase its exposure excessively on this type of opportunity? Is it reasonable?

After determining the desired global exposure (10%, 5%, 2%), the trader will have to divide his capital in different positions. However, it is possible to allocate the same amount (in the capital and in maximum loss) for each position initiated. The main criticism of this approach is that it assumes that all operations present similar opportunities, which is rarely the case.

Finally, another important element is the correlation between the different securities in the portfolio. Two titles are positively correlated if their evolution is similar. Generally, securities in the same sector move in the same direction. A trader who has highly correlated securities in his portfolio is therefore exposed to significant risks that only diversification can mitigate by decreasing the volatility of the portfolio. In return, the trader will have to accept lower performance.

## Peer Trading

This technique is used by many hedge funds and traders in the trading room. It offers a way to reduce risk by taking two opposing positions on two positively correlated products (for example shares in the same sector). The purpose of this operation is to take advantage of the relative difference in the adjustment between the two financial products.

If a trader believes that Peugeot is undervalued compared to Renault, he can buy Peugeot and sell the Renault to take advantage of this temporary valuation gap. Here, the trader will not try to predict whether Peugeot will go up or down but is based primarily on the relative evolution of Peugeot compared to Renault. Both stocks may fall but this will have no impact on his performance since the gain on Renault (a title he sells) should be offset by the loss recorded on Peugeot (a title he buys). This transaction considers that the loss will be largely offset by the gain and will generate a profit. The purpose of the spread is to reduce the risk related to a forecast error and to base its decision on the valuation difference between two assets.

The advantage of this approach is that the trader is not a victim of market risk - an unexpected rise or fall in the market will have no impact on his position since the loss on an asset (linked to a random event) will be offset by the gain on the other asset assumed to move in the same direction. This technique requires significant funds and low brokerage fees, but it can lead to significant gains for those who control it.

# The Limits of Diversification

Diversification reduces the risk associated with trading but cannot completely eliminate it. Indeed, there is always a portfolio risk that cannot be eliminated despite diversification. In the same way, diversification diminishes the trader's attention and does not allow him to make the most of his positions. This strategy will depend heavily on the fund's philosophy and time horizon. We will privilege for the short term a specialization of the trader on some titles and for the swing traders a specialization on some sectors or markets.

# How to Select a Powerful Trading System?

According to J. Welles Wilder, most financial assets evolve in trend 30% of the time. The rest of the time, the markets evolve laterally, that is, no clear trend is detectable. The trader will have to adapt his method to the type of market as well as the current trend. The ideal for a trader is to work in a trending market. Indeed, it is difficult to make money in markets without trend because of brokerage fees and the need for the trader to be constantly in the markets. The trader will have to select first the markets offering the most beautiful configurations, and then make a ranking opportunity offering the best opportunities, according to an order of preference. However, this remark does not apply to traders who favor short-term techniques (day trading and scalping). Good traders will proceed as follows:

Firstly, they will identify several markets trend or about to enter the trend phase; select from those markets those with the highest potential and with little or no correlation with others.

Choose one with a high Sharpe ratio. William Sharpe has done a study on the performance of mutual funds in the United States. He put forward the idea that risk-adjusted portfolio return was a significant measure of performance. He created the ratio that bears his name: It goes without saying that it is better to have a smooth performance indicating the regularity of the trader and therefore the elimination of the random phenomena of his performance. A chaotic performance means that the investor is subject to significant risk, that its performance may be by chance and that the risk of ruin is high. A portfolio with a high return and extreme volatility is a danger.

The trader will have to select the trading system with the highest Sharpe ratio. For example, he will be able to analyze a system that he has used in the past and will rely on the history of his performance. He will also be able to evaluate a trading system (not yet used but derived from his research) thanks to the Sharpe ratio.

# A Powerful but Simple Trading System

The trader has every interest in opting for a simple system whose rules he rules, rather than for a more efficient system (on paper) but whose rules are complex.

Indeed, there is a good chance that the trader does not respect his plan, especially with a sophisticated trading system, because his emotions will quickly take over. On the markets, there is no room for hesitation and it is decisive for a trader to be convinced of the veracity of his system and especially to control it well. To be operational, a system will have to prove its effectiveness in the facts. A system will never be fixed or fixed once and for all, and the trader will proceed by trial and error at first. With experience, the trader can sophisticate his system.

We are convinced that it is preferable to have an imperfect but simple system rather than a system that is efficient on paper but complex and therefore difficult to implement: the financial markets have the power to destabilize traders and this deal will have to be imperative. Be taken into account when developing the trading system.

# Some Techniques to Improve Its Performance

In this part, we will study the swing trading system and we will see to what extent it is often successful. We will also study the classic system used by most novice traders and we will highlight its weaknesses.

The swing trading system means "in the direction of the dominant movement". This system, often used by traders, allows testing the market before increasing its exposure. Indeed, if the market confirms the trader's initial scenario, it is because his reasoning is good, and he can, by crossing some pivotal points, strengthen his position. This system was successfully used by one of the greatest speculators of the last century and is described in his book.

# Conclusion

Thank you for making it through to the end of *Options Trading 2*, let's hope it was informative and able to provide you with all of the tools you need to achieve your goals whatever they may be.

You've now had a careful stroll through the key standards and ventures in options trading we feel are fundamental to progress as an options trader. You've figured out how the options markets function, the best trading strategies and why it's basic to pick the best possible fundamental assets for the procedures you need to utilize. You've additionally observed that great exit strategies are nearly as imperative as discovering great trades to enter, that focusing on the points of interest is basic, and that achievement is virtually inconceivable without a decent money-management plan—and the discipline to follow it.

At last, you've got lots of pages loaded with vital inquiries to consider in your search for the best online options broker. At the end of the day, it's a great opportunity to control up, plugin—and profit. You have all the data you have to appreciate 24-hour access to the options markets, fast and programmed execution of your orders and the most reduced commissions in the history of options trading. In any case, to share these advantages, you should confront the lot bigger individual duties that accompany coordinate access online trading.

You should have the discipline to do your very own research, screen your own positions and monitor every one of the points of interest you may leave to your full-benefit financial firm. You can never again depend on a broker to watch your positions and call with guidance or suggestions. You are currently an autonomous administrator — and, all things considered, must be absolutely in charge of your own behavior.

You should likewise be mindful and be prepared to react to both fast moves in everyday trading designs and consistently evolving longer-term economic situations.

A Dose of Reality to Induce Caution . . .

In case you think tolerating such difficulties and practicing such discipline is simple, think of one as a little preventative portion of the real world. An investigation—"Online Investors: Do the Slow Die First?" by Brad M. Barber and Terrance Odean, published in Economic Intuition,

Spring 2000—discovered that: "Online trading makes a deception of information that really gives traders less profit for their investments. While online-trader certainty ascends with extra data, exactness does not. Accordingly, traders are more averse to make a profit on every transaction—and will make less profit on successful transactions. Statistically, online traders:

- Trade 96 percent more as often as possible than telephone-based traders.
- Are twice as speculative online as they are with their disconnected trades.
- Produce overall returns that slack the market returns by 3.4 to 4.0 percent, notwithstanding when figuring in the lower commission costs. "In this manner, while full-benefit commissions can be costly, they're for the most part justified, in light of the additional experience and alert that brokers add to the trading procedure."

. . . A Final Dose of Reassurance

That is a calming bit of research, and way back 2000—and I concur that a specific level of caution is something to be thankful for. Notwithstanding, we stay persuaded that you can be an accomplisher as an options trader. For a thing, the investigation above depended on stock trading, not options trading—and the proficiency differential among online and stock trading is far, way lower than between electronic and conventional options trading.

The same is valid for commissions—which, not long ago, have been a lot higher on a percentage basis for options, than stocks.

Immediate online access to prices, the accessibility of enhanced analytical tools, including screening programs, and the simplicity of utilizing stops and limit orders additionally have an altogether more positive effect on options traders than on stock buyers. As it were, the variations are substantial to the point that we'll utilize them as a reason to repeat the argument we made in the Introduction: "In the event that You Haven't Traded Options, You Haven't Really Traded." what's more, the stock traders overviewed by Barder and Odean didn't have the advantage of the abundance of data you've recently read.

Furthermore, we're not through yet! As a last note, I would like to ask for one more thing from you. That is a solid dedication on your part to observe the following five rules and regulations—rules we promise will significantly improve your chances of getting to be an accomplished online options trader, as well as an accomplished investor generally speaking.

They are:

1. **Give option trading a reasonable chance—no less than a whole year.** Regardless of whether your initial three or four trades result in losses, that is not an excuse to surrender and cash in your chips. By then, despite everything, you're beginning to understand the complexities of the online system and honoring your

market skills. If you encounter a couple of losses initially, simply reduce the extent of your trades—for example, stop ordering 10-contract positions and begin ordering single, three or five options. Keep your size low until the point when you begin to get few losers and more winners—at that point return to greater positions once more. In that manner, you'll save your underlying stake and allow yourself to make right an amateur's mistakes—or, to ride out your present losing streak if you're more of a veteran.

2. **Avoid spreading yourself too thin.** Rather than wanting to move from index to index, or stock to stock, looking for the "most blazing" option openings, monitor a limited number of basic stocks and just a single or two market indexes. Focus on following the news and financial numbers on your picked issues, and soon, you will realize what in general trigger price moves — and when they're probably to happen. At that point, you'll realize the best periods to start the suitable option trades.

3. **Are you brave enough to accept the loss?** Even the most accomplished option professionals don't make a profit on all trades, be ready to get out of a terrible position when you notice it. That is the initial phase in finding the next incredible chance. Furthermore, come what may occur in the market, NEVER move a stop so you won't be presented to a bigger loss. That is the initial

phase in finishing your trading profession—and finishing it terribly.

4. **Try not to give achievement a chance to make you presumptuous—or far more terrible, selfish.** When you manufacture your account equity to a decent working dimension, begin moving a segment of your future profits into less-speculative investments. For instance, if you begin with $20,000 or less, keep 100 percent of your profits working until the point when you manufacture your equity to $50,000. At that point begin moving no less than 25 percent of your trading profits into better secure investments, giving 75 percent a chance to keep working— until the point when you reach $100,000. At that point, put 50 percent of new profits aside for more conservative interests. If you feel constrained to keep 100 percent of your profits working constantly, you'll most likely end up being presented to risk more—which means one snappy string of awful trades could clear all your previous gains.

DO take the full preferred standpoint of what you've realized in this book. Begin shopping for your very own online broker and options trading program today!

Finally, if you found this book useful in any way, a review on Amazon is always appreciated!